Self-Assessment and Training

Self-Assessment and Training

Guidelines for Pedagogical Supervision

Yamina Bouchamma,
Marc Giguère, and Daniel April

ROWMAN & LITTLEFIELD
Lanham • Boulder • New York • London

Published by Rowman & Littlefield
An imprint of The Rowman & Littlefield Publishing Group, Inc.
4501 Forbes Boulevard, Suite 200, Lanham, Maryland 20706
www.rowman.com

6 Tinworth Street, London SE11 5AL, United Kingdom

British Library Cataloguing in Publication Information Available

Library of Congress Cataloging-in-Publication Data Is Available

ISBN 978-1-4758-5098-7 (cloth: alk. paper)
ISBN 978-1-4758-5099-4 (pbk: alk. paper)
ISBN 978-1-4758-5100-7 (electronic)

Contents

List of Figures and Tables

Introduction

In the context of the accountability that governs the schools today, pedagogical supervision has become more than ever unavoidable. Because of its control function, which in some respects approximates evaluation, supervision is likely to cause concern and mistrust, and in some cases, school-team members could refuse to comply with it. This is an operation that must involve the many stakeholders (the Department of Education, school boards, principals, and teachers) and take into account different dimensions (educational, legal, political, socioeconomic, and emotional).

In fact, pedagogical supervision has evolved over time and different models have been used by principals (Bouchamma, 2005). Over the last few years, supervision has often been done through professional learning communities (PLCs). This mode of operation has created a renewed interest in supervision. Through PLCs, principals and teaching and nonteaching staff work collectively to improve students' academic success.

This book follows the first volume, *Pedagogical Supervision: A Competency Standards Framework*. Chapters 1, 2, and 3 review respectively the concept of competency, the concept of pedagogical supervision, and the skills of the pedagogical supervisor. These skills are classified according to these four competence areas:

- *knowledge (know-what)*;
- *know how to do*;
- *know how to be*; and
- *know how to become*.

This book and this research-action training ("Améliorer les compétences des gestionnaires d'établissement scolaire en supervision pédagogique par la communauté d'apprentissage et de pratique professionnelle en présentiel et en ligne" [Bouchamma & Giguère, 2014–2017]) were supported by the Québec Ministry of Education (in-service training program for school staff).

Chapter One

Come Back to the Concept of "Competency"

In the previous volume, *Pedagogical Supervision: A Competency Standards Framework*, we adopted the following definition of the concept of competency:

> Competence is a complex *know-how-to-act* in a concrete professional context. It pertains to the ability to mobilize a group of interdependent forms of knowledge, namely, know-what (knowledge), know-how-to-do (skills), know-how-to-be (attitudes), and know-how-to-become (professional development) to ensure competent actions. It emerges from an intention (wanting to act) and from available resources (being able to act). Competent action refers to accomplishing a task or operation, performing a duty, or achieving a goal based on established expectations and anticipated outcomes.

Knowledge, knowing how to do, knowing how to be, and *knowing how to become* make up a series of interdependent dimensions integrated within this definition of competence:

Table 1.1. Definitions of *Knowledge, Know How to Do, Know How to Be,* and *Know How to Become*

Knowledge (know-what):	Refers to cognitive knowledge obtained through formal or informal training and certification.
Know how to do:	Refers to the ability to enable the transfer from theory to practice.
Know how to be:	Refers to how a professional views themselves within the realm of values, attitudes, and behaviors in terms of context, their position within this context, their personal reaction to problems, and, lastly, regarding others. Knowing how to be makes it possible to use our personal resources (aptitudes, qualities, emotions, or physiological attributes) in a given situation.
Know how to become:	Refers to the manner in which a professional engages individually and collectively within a continuous and sustainable process of self-development and mobility.

Figure 1.1, taken from the previous volume (*Pedagogical Supervision*), schematically illustrates the concept of competence.

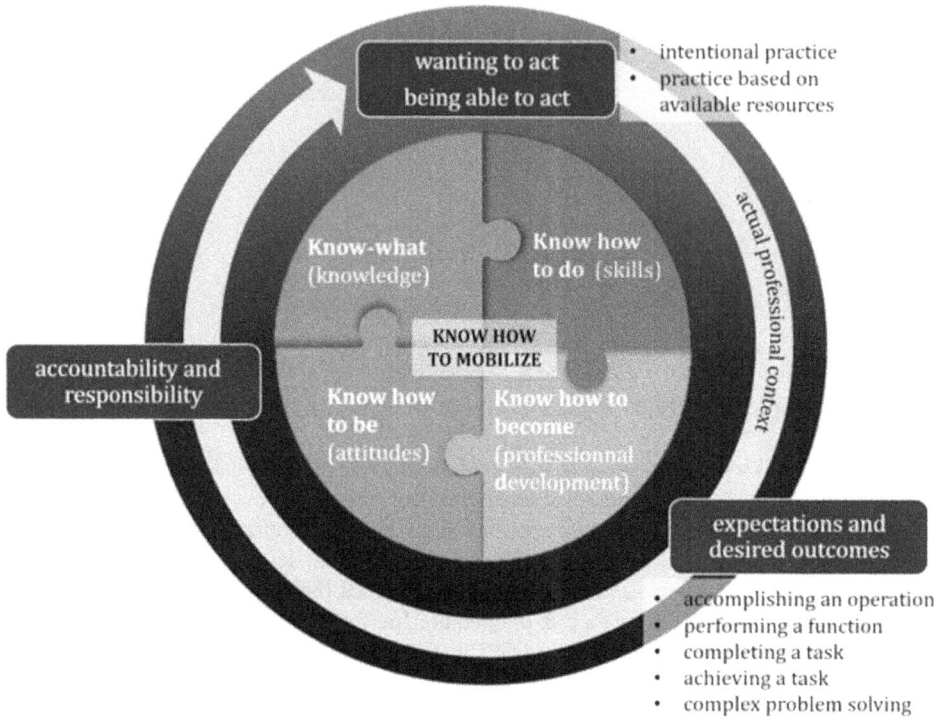

Figure 1.1.   The Definition of Competence

Chapter Two

Come Back to the Concept of "Pedagogical Supervision"

In the previous volume, *Pedagogical Supervision*, we adopted the following definition of the concept of supervision, which takes place on different levels, with each level feeding the next level in a systemic manner:

> Pedagogical supervision is an approach characterized by discussions with and support for a person or group of persons. A critical analysis is performed during ongoing actions or processes on one of the following aspects:
>
> - the education services provided by the staff;
> - the organization's priorities;
> - the actions inherent to an operation, group of operations, or mandate;
> - the pedagogical projects developed within the organization;
> - the work performed in a perspective of professional development; or others.

Pedagogical supervision aims to enhance ongoing processes and actions and to introduce the necessary changes to attain the desired outcomes. The point of pedagogical supervision is thus to improve the educational services for the students and the latter's qualitative and quantitative achievement.

The following figure reproduced from the previous volume, *Pedagogical Supervision*, summarizes the concept of pedagogical supervision based on five dimensions: prerequisites, who, what, for whom, and why. The supervisor (who) must first establish a climate of trust and discussion (prerequisites). The latter then undertakes supervision actions (what) with the supervised person (for whom) with the ultimate goal of improving student outcomes (why).

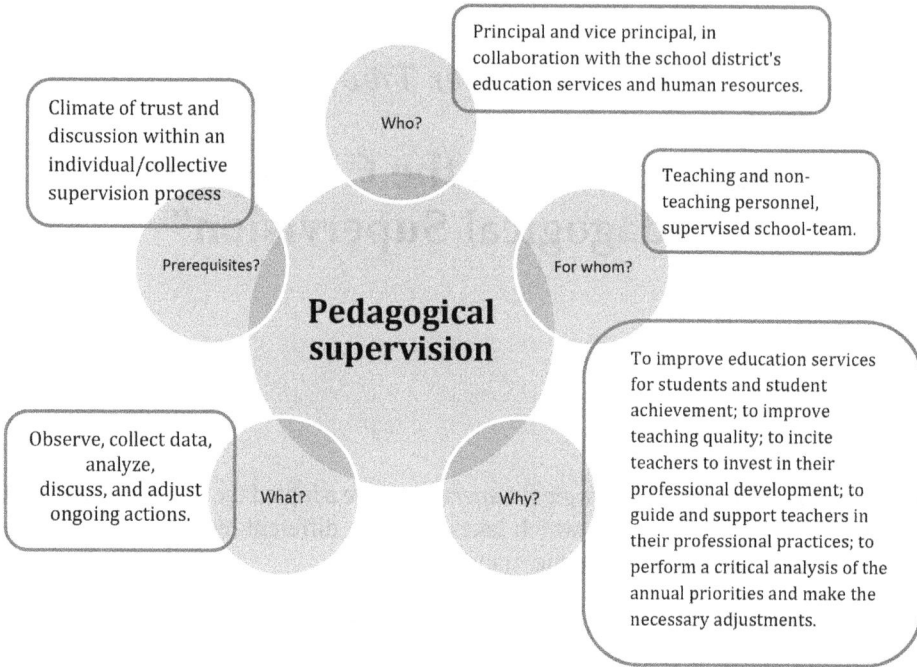

Principal and vice principal, in collaboration with the school district's education services and human resources.

Climate of trust and discussion within an individual/collective supervision process

Who?

Teaching and non-teaching personnel, supervised school-team.

Prerequisites?

For whom?

Pedagogical supervision

To improve education services for students and student achievement; to improve teaching quality; to incite teachers to invest in their professional development; to guide and support teachers in their professional practices; to perform a critical analysis of the annual priorities and make the necessary adjustments.

Observe, collect data, analyze, discuss, and adjust ongoing actions.

What?

Why?

Figure 2.1.   Overview of Pedagogical Supervision

Chapter Three

Come Back to the Skills
of the Pedagogical Supervisor

In the previous volume, *Pedagogical Supervision*, we defined the two types of competencies in pedagogical supervision (see Table 3.1).

Table 3.1.   Definitions of Pedagogical Skills and Human Relation Skills

Pedagogical skills:	Aims to improve the practices and educational services (by encouraging the professional and pedagogical development of the school-team and by perfecting educational actions) toward the improvement of student outcomes.
Human relation skills:	Aims to favor relationships with, between, and among the teachers and to establish a relationship of trust and collaboration between several individuals or groups of individuals. Involve three abilities related to emotional intelligence: self-esteem, self-control, and social conscience. These skills enhance clarity in what is being communicated.

We have also defined six transversal or core skills in pedagogical supervision (see Table 3.2).

Table 3.2.   Definitions of the Six Transversal Skills in Pedagogical Supervision

Leadership:	Ability to have a clear vision of the changes to be undertaken coupled with the ability to influence and lead others toward this vision.
Method:	Rigorously structured mode of operation to solve problems (transfer of each skill in every situation involving supervision) and get results. The method requires data collection, the determination of priorities, elaboration and implementation, and the supervision and evaluation of an action plan.
Cooperation:	Cooperation occurs in the form of connections and behaviors through which a relationship is created between supervisor and the supervised person to enable harmonious exchange and the identification, together, of the appropriate means to move toward effective solutions.

(Continued)

Table 3.2. *(Continued)*

Communication:	Refers to the emission and reception of messages that carry meaning between the supervisor and the supervised person. Each behavior has the value of a message. The supervisor establishes good communication by ensuring the construction of a common meaning and language and the sharing of their vision.
Ethics:	Moral principles that govern the supervisor's behavior. A good supervisor establishes a management culture founded on transparency, accountability, impartiality, and responsibility.
Emotional intelligence:	Capacity to understand our own self and effectively manage our own emotions and relationships with others.

Figure 3.1 illustrates the two types of skills of a pedagogical supervisor and the six core skills mentioned above.

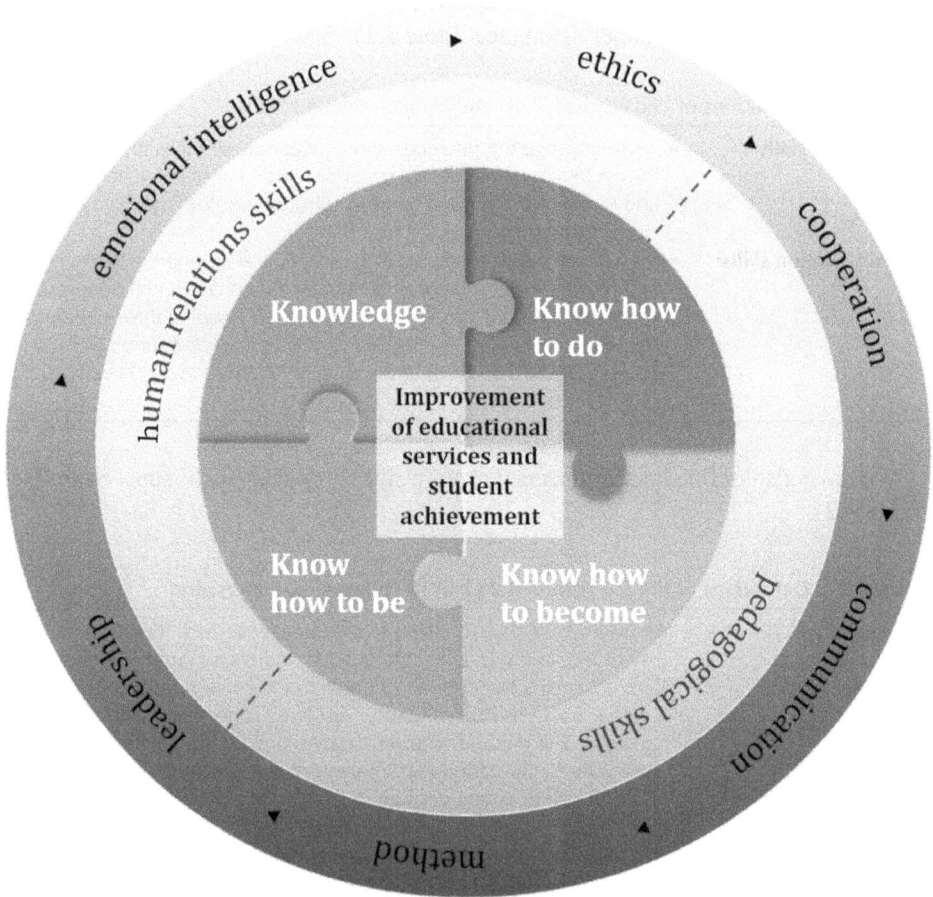

Figure 3.1.   Essential Skills of a Pedagogical Supervisor

Table 3.3 presents all of the knowledge, *know how to do*, *know how to be*, and *know how to become* examined in the previous volume, *Pedagogical Supervision*.

Table 3.3. Competencies of the Effective Supervisor

Knowledge	
Pedagogically	*In Human Relations*
4.1.1 Have a pedagogical vision and educational values.	4.2.1 Know the organizational culture and particularities of my work environment.
4.1.2 Know the national and local policies pertaining to teacher supervision.	4.2.2 Know the personal and professional profile of each supervised teacher.
4.1.3 Know my school's issues regarding student achievement.	4.2.3 Know my leadership and management styles.
4.1.4 Know the resources provided by Education Services to support my teacher supervision practice.	4.2.4 Know the services provided by Human Resources to support my teacher supervision practice.
4.1.5 Know the basic principles of pedagogical supervision.	4.2.5 Know facilitation techniques
Know How to Do	
Pedagogically	*In Human Relations*
Leadership: 5.1.1 Use pedagogical leadership: Promote my vision of the school system, my educational orientations and values; encourage the professional development of my staff; support pedagogical projects and innovations. 5.1.2 Use situational leadership: Focus on the students' needs and the school's education priorities. 5.1.3 Manage ethnocultural diversity in my school. **Method:** 5.1.4 Organize my time to make teacher supervision a priority. 5.1.5 Supervise the attainment of the achievement objectives. 5.1.6 Encourage and support the pedagogical projects of my teachers and assist them in their professional development related to the school's priorities and the students' needs.	**Leadership:** 5.2.1 Use relational leadership: Encourage communication, consultation, and discussion among the teachers. 5.2.2 Use transformational leadership: Inspire, stimulate, optimize the potential of each teacher, and empower them toward self-reliance. 5.2.3 Delegate support duties and responsibilities to the vice principal and to teachers and closely monitor. 5.2.4 Maintain staff awareness of the main orientations and general objectives regarding student achievement. **Method:** 5.2.5 Objectively analyze the school's climate. 5.2.6 Develop and implement a pluriannual supervision plan for my teachers.

(Continued)

Table 3.3. *(Continued)*

Pedagogically	*In Human Relations*
5.1.7 Supervise the compliance to national/local policies and those of the school in matters of pedagogy.	5.2.7 Use data collection and analysis tools.
	5.2.8 Agree to the mutual expectations during the individual/group supervision process.
5.1.8 Financially support my teachers' pedagogical projects and professional development needs.	5.2.9 Guide each supervised teacher to self-evaluate and set professional growth objectives.
5.1.9 Structure organization to enable teachers to attend professional development activities.	5.2.10 Provide constructive individual/group feedback following supervision activities and follow up accordingly.
5.1.10 Perform teacher supervision with no subjectivity.	**Cooperation:** 5.2.11 Consult school district services for specific expertise.
Cooperation: 5.1.11 Establish work groups/PLCs in my school and encourage peer collaboration.	**Communication:** 5.2.12 Communicate clearly with my teachers.
5.1.12 Assist my school-team in finding and applying the most effective educational practices for the specific needs of the students.	**Ethics:** 5.2.13 Encourage and organize development activities based on the school's needs and those of the teachers.
	5.2.14 Use differentiated supervision for behaviors related to the motivation, commitment, and professional competence of the supervised teacher.
	5.2.15 Ensure that the rules of confidentiality are respected.
	5.2.16 Acknowledge the personal/collective contributions and successes of my teachers.
	5.2.17 Demonstrate managerial courage in certain supervision situations.
	5.2.18 Declare my intentions and explain my supervision actions.

Know How to Be	
Pedagogically	*In Human Relations*
Ethics: 6.1.1 Be consistent in my educational values and my professional practice.	**Method:** 6.2.1 Be flexible and available.
6.1.2 Welcome pedagogical initiatives.	**Cooperation:** 6.2.2 Be sociable.
	Ethics: 6.2.3 Be fair.

Pedagogically	*In Human Relations*
	6.2.4 Believe in the progress and professional development of each supervised person.
	Emotional intelligence:
	6.2.5 Possess a strong sense of personal efficacy.
	6.2.6 Manage my stress and emotions.
	6.2.7 Consider the emotional and affective dimension of the supervised person and show empathy.
	6.2.8 Be a good listener.
	6.2.9 Make people comfortable and trusting.

Know How to Become	
Pedagogically	*In Human Relations*
7.1.1 Self-evaluate and identify my training needs in pedagogy and supervision.	7.2.1 Learn more about human relations approaches.
7.1.2 Learn more about pedagogical innovations and winning trends in this field.	
7.1.3 Develop my professional development program in pedagogy.	
7.1.4 Keep abreast of new theories and practices in teacher supervision	

Chapter Four

The Knowledge for Effective Supervision

4.1—PEDAGOGICAL KNOWLEDGE

In this section, we examine five pedagogical skills:

- Have a pedagogical vision and educational values.
- Know the national and local policies pertaining to teacher supervision.
- Know my school's issues regarding student achievement.
- Know the resources provided by Education Services to support my teacher supervision practice.
- Know the basic principles of pedagogical supervision.

4.1.1—Have a Pedagogical Vision and Educational Values

What the Supervisors Say

Effective supervisors emphasize the importance of having your own educational values:

- "As principal, I have to have my own pedagogical orientations and educational values that correspond to what I want to convey within my school." (Principal, Elementary)

- "If you don't have your own personal educational values and well-thought-out pedagogical orientations, take the time to think about that; it's crucial for anyone who is principal." (Principal, Elementary)

- "I have my own educational values and pedagogical aspirations, but I must hold true to those of my school's Education Plan." (Principal, Elementary)

How far do these testimonials reflect your experiences? (See Table 4.1.)

Table 4.1.   Self-Evaluation: Have a Pedagogical Vision and Educational Values

	Yes	Sometimes	No	Does not apply
1. I have a pedagogical vision (orientations) for my school, and I convey it to the educators in my school.				
2. I have educational values that guide my professional actions.				
3. I prioritize the educational values of my school when they are not the same as mine in every aspect.				
4. I am capable of looking ahead with regard to the pedagogical orientations of my school system.				
5. I recognize why it is important that my administrative decisions be driven by sanctioned pedagogical orientations.				
6. My vision of supervision centers on the educational values of my school.				
7. My vision of supervision centers on the orientations and official general objectives of my school.				
Others:				

What actions should I undertake to develop a pedagogical vision (orientations) and to better convey my educational values?

Exercise 1—Educational Values and Pedagogical Vision

1. Name the main educational values that best interest you.
2. Explain the pedagogical vision (orientations) you would like to establish in your school.

4.1.2—Know the National and Local Policies Pertaining to Teacher Supervision

What the Supervisors Say

According to the successful supervisors in our research-action-training project, it is the duty of the supervisor to apply all ministerial directives in their school:

- "It is the Ministry of Education's job to determine the broad orientations of the school system and our job to apply them in our schools." (Principal, Elementary)

Although they require a minimal amount of knowledge in various fields of expertise (law, e.g.), supervisors do not know everything; for this reason, they do not hesitate to seek the support of the appropriate services in their district when necessary:

- "I can't be a lawyer, an engineer, an architect. . . . I'm an educator. When I need help, I call upon the services of the school district who are specialists in the field." (Principal, Secondary)

- "It's not necessary to know every article in the collective agreement; I learn the most important ones and for the rest, I refer to Human Resources." (Principal, Elementary)

- "The guidelines determine which actions are a priority. However, the annual evaluation does give us a bit of leeway to integrate new ideas." (Principal, Adult Education)

How far do these testimonials reflect your experiences? (See Table 4.2.)

Table 4.2. Self-Evaluation: Know the National and Local Policies Pertaining to Teacher Supervision

	Yes	Sometimes	No	Does not apply
I possess the necessary knowledge/information regarding . . .				
1. the relevant legislation on teacher supervision.				
2. the government policies that affect my teacher supervision (e.g., inclusion of students with learning or behavior difficulties, learning assessments, etc.).				
3. the main elements of the collective agreements.				
4. the directives of my school: its specific orientations and general objectives to improve student achievement;				
its annual action plan (means to achieve our goals);				
its rules of conduct and security measures for the students;				
its policies and regulations.				
Others:				

What strategies should I adopt to develop my knowledge and understanding of the national and local policies pertaining to teacher supervision?

4.1.3—Know My School's Issues Regarding Student Achievement

What the Supervisors Say

Understanding the school's issues helps to determine goals for student achievement:

- "It's important to know where my students are at in their learning process. It enables me and my school-team to set achievement objectives and focus on the teaching practices we should work on." (Principal, Elementary)

- "One of my strengths is being able to identify the issues that affect us the most, what we do in our everyday lives. I think that it's something that stands out. It helps me to set goals for our specific context and to measure the attainment of these goals." (Principal, Adult General Education)

How far do these testimonials reflect your experiences? (See Table 4.3.)

Table 4.3.   Self-Evaluation: Know My School's Issues Regarding Student Achievement

	Yes	Sometimes	No	Does not apply
I possess the necessary knowledge/information regarding . . .				
1. the context in which my school evolves.				
2. the main issues of my school regarding student achievement.				
3. the means established to attain our objectives.				
4. the indicators used to measure the attainment of the targeted objectives.				
5. the factors explaining my students' outcomes.				
6. my students' outcomes on government assessments.				
7. my students' rate of achievement after each reporting period of the year.				
Others:				

What strategies should I develop to better understand my school's issues regarding student achievement?

4.1.4—Know the Resources Provided by Education Services to Support My Teacher Supervision Practice

What the Supervisors Say

A good supervisor knows the limits of their pedagogical expertise and welcomes the support of education consultants:

- "I can't answer all of the questions on what's in the education programs; in such cases, I put my teacher in contact with the education consultant specialized in their discipline." (Principal, Elementary)

- "Education consultants are not in charge of pedagogy in my school, but they can counsel us, help us, and support us. That's how I see their role." (Principal, Elementary)

How far do these testimonials reflect your experiences? (See Table 4.4.)

Table 4.4. Self-Evaluation: Know the Resources Provided by Education Services to Support My Teacher Supervision Practice (adapted from Houle & Pratte, 2003)

	Yes	Sometimes	No	Does not apply
For *my teachers*, whether individually or as a group, I use the services of education consultants because they . . .				
1. provide pedagogical expertise for my teachers.				
2. provide didactic expertise relative to their disciplinary field.				
3. use their pedagogical resources (expertise) to serve my school.				
4. contribute to pedagogical development in my school.				
5. accompany new teachers in their chosen discipline, when necessary.				
6. provide counsel regarding the pedagogical development and disciplines of my teachers.				

(Continued)

Table 4.4.   *(Continued)*

	Yes	Sometimes	No	Does not apply
7. assist in the implementation of a pedagogical reform in my school.				
8. counsel my teachers on which didactic materials to use.				
9. contribute to the development of education programs (elaboration, training, implementation, evaluation).				
For *myself, as supervisor,* I use the services of education consultants because they . . .				
10. act as pedagogical leader (convey orientations, initiate projects, mobilize).				
11. develop training activities.				
12. provide counsel on collaborations with other schools.				
Others:				

What strategies should I develop to better understand the resources provided by Education Services to support my teacher supervision practice?

4.1.5—Know the Basic Principles of Pedagogical Supervision

What the Supervisors Say

First and foremost, the possible hesitance toward/rejection of supervision may arise from the confusion between the notions of *evaluation* and *supervision*. Indeed, the following statements appear to support the fact that teachers are not at all against their professional development:

- "When we say supervision, we easily think of evaluation. When we speak of supervision in the sense of continuing education, support, and guidance, it [will win]. No one wants to stagnate; everyone wants to improve." (Principal, Elementary)

- "Could it be that the greatest obstacle to teacher supervision is the ignorance of our teachers or their misconception of the term 'evaluation' and that the unions take advantage of this to portray us as the bad guy?" (Principal, Secondary)

How far do these testimonials reflect your experiences? (See Table 4.5.)

Table 4.5. Self-Evaluation: Know the Basic Principles of Pedagogical Supervision
(adapted from Bouchamma, Iancu, & Stanescu, 2008)

	Yes	Sometimes	No	Does not apply
I know the definition, extent, and particularities of individual supervision.				
1. I understand its meaning, and I know the difference between it and evaluation.				
2. I know that I must first establish a relationship of trust with my supervised teacher.				
3. I know that above all, it must correspond to: their profile (personal/professional);				
the context in which it takes place.				
4. I know that other actors may participate in the professional development of the supervised teacher (mentoring, student feedback, peer sponsorship).				
I know what steps to take in the first supervision interview.				
Before the interview . . .				
5. I explain the objectives of the meeting to the supervised teacher.				
6. I give them the tools that will be used during the interview.				
During the interview . . .				
7. I make sure that the supervised teacher feels comfortable.				
8. I remind them of the objectives of the supervision and the interview.				
9. I listen to their expectations.				
10. We decide which elements are to be addressed in the supervision.				
11. We analyze the tools that will be used in the following stages of the supervision.				
12. We determine how we will proceed: in-class observations, feedback, and final interview.				
I know the steps to follow to perform a good observation (before, during, and after).				
Before the observation visit . . .				
13. I meet with the supervised teacher to determine the aspect(s) targeted by the observation.				

(Continued)

Table 4.5. *(Continued)*

	Yes	Sometimes	No	Does not apply
14. We decide when the observation will take place.				
15. We discuss the preparation.				
16. I share with the supervised teacher the grids I use during my in-class observation.				
During the observation visit . . .				
17. I collect the data using the grids I shared with the supervised teacher.				
18. I am discreet during my observation.				
Following the observation visit . . .				
19. I ask for their self-evaluation.				
20. I guide them to reflect on their practices.				
21. I interactively share my comments with them based on their self-evaluation and the observed actions.				
22. I interactively point out the adjustments to be made for the next supervision.				
23. We discuss professional development opportunities.				
24. We agree on a continuing education activity that is compatible with their needs and transferable to their in-class practice.				
25. I encourage them to discuss their teaching practices with others (peers, education consultants, etc.).				
26. I request a written or verbal report on the training received following a professional development activity.				
Others:				

What strategies should I adopt to better understand the basic principles of pedagogical supervision?

4.2—KNOWLEDGE IN HUMAN RELATIONS

In this section, we examine five elements of knowledge in human relations:

- Know the organizational culture and particularities of my work environment.
- Know the personal and professional profile of each supervised teacher.
- Know my leadership and management styles.
- Know the services provided by Human Resources to support my teacher supervision practice.
- Know facilitation techniques.

4.2.1—Know the Organizational Culture and Particularities of My Work Environment

What the Supervisors Say

Winning supervisors agree that before implementation is undertaken, their pedagogical supervision must meet certain requirements that are coherent with the school's organizational culture.

- "Before working on the supervision, I'm going to find out more about my school's organizational culture and in particular how the union feels about supervision." (Principal, Secondary)

These leaders are conscious of the extreme importance of collecting field data, which should in fact be the starting point of every good supervision initiative:

- "Talking to the students, asking why, and not just in my team of teachers, but getting feedback from the students to help us find the right ways to do things differently. I exploited this a lot lately and I got a few surprises through that. It's an ongoing process. It's a strategy to understand the student culture in my school. Going to meet the student council. . . . Walking around my school more. Going into the classrooms. . . . I saw some extraordinary things, but I also witnessed some things that will have to be worked on in terms of supervision—that's for sure, sure, sure." (Principal, Secondary)

There are also culture differences between elementary and secondary education levels:

- "The professional culture in elementary school is not the same as the one in high school. You have to adapt your interventions to fit the profile of the teachers you supervise." (Principal, Secondary)

Supervisors must therefore be flexible by adapting their strategies to fit the context:

- "Even teachers in Secondary Cycle 1 don't react the same as those in Cycle 2 do. You've got to adapt your strategies accordingly." (Vice Principal, Secondary)

How far do these testimonials reflect your experiences? (See Table 4.6.)

Table 4.6. Self-Evaluation: Know the Organizational Culture and Particularities of My Work Environment

	Yes	Sometimes	No	Does not apply
I rely on documents and statistics to know . . .				
My school:				
1. Its history;				
2. Its most significant positive events (students' achievement over time, sports-related achievements, cultural exploits, etc.);				
3. Its most significant negative events (suicide, violence, etc.).				
Others:				
My district:				
4. Its particularities in terms of its composition (homogeneity/ heterogeneity, immigration, deprivation index), its assets, issues, level of involvement in school activities.				
Others:				
I rely on information from direct sources (meetings with the student council, in-school observations, short anonymous student surveys, etc.) and indirect sources (discussions with teaching and nonteaching staff) to know . . .				
The students:				
5. The culture of my students (values, achievement, sense of belonging, etc.).				
Others:				
I rely on individual/group, formal/informal discussions with my teachers to know . . .				
The teachers:				
6. Their beliefs and values regarding the academic success of their students;				
7. Their beliefs and values regarding teacher supervision;				
8. The "union view" of my teachers regarding teacher supervision;				
9. The level of trust my teachers sense with me.				
Others:				

	Yes	Sometimes	No	Does not apply
10. I make it a point to remind my staff of significant positive events as a mobilization strategy.				
11. I am on the lookout for ways to avoid the emergence of other negative events.				
Others:				

What actions should I undertake to better understand the organizational culture and particularities of my work environment?

4.2.2—Know the Personal and Professional Profile of Each Supervised Teacher

What the Supervisors Say

Successful supervisors recognize the benefits of knowing their supervised teachers, both personally and professionally, as this knowledge facilitates communication:

- "I make it a point to know a few personal things about my supervised teachers because it makes the approach easier. As for the professional aspects, I have to have information regarding their teaching." (Principal, Elementary)

The supervisor/supervised teacher relationship resembles the teacher/student dynamic in that it favors a good classroom climate:

- "It's like a teacher with their students; the teacher must know them to be able to establish a good working relationship in class." (Vice Principal, Elementary)

This knowledge between supervisor and supervised teacher is also reciprocal and is not limited to the professional level but also involves personal aspects:

- "There are many other sources other than the school to explain how I know my people. They know me too. I don't just talk about school with my staff." (Principal, Elementary)

For some, the starting point may be, for example, a teacher's hobby:

- "My winning practice is: Start with what interests them. . . . You have to know their interests and what motivates them." (Principal, Vocational Education)

Drawing on the strengths of the team is also a winning strategy, particularly when the words reflect the actions:

- "My action plan is based on the team's strengths. There is consistency in the words and in the actions." (Principal, Secondary)

How far do these testimonials reflect your experiences? (See Tables 4.7 and 4.8.)

Table 4.7. Self-Evaluation: Know the Personal and Professional Profile of Each Supervised Teacher (adapted from Girard, McLean, & Morissette, 1992)

	Yes	*Sometimes*	*No*	*Does not apply*
My supervised teacher understands . . .				
1. supervision and what it entails.				
2. the conditions that favor human interactions.				
3. education programs and what is expected of these programs.				
4. teaching theories (pedagogical differentiation).				
5. learning theories (socioconstructivism).				
6. the theories on evaluation practices (formative, summative).				
7. their students: their history, their profile.				
8. how to meet their needs: facilitating: knowing how groups work; using specific approaches depending on their age and particularities, type of group.				
My supervised teacher knows how to . . .				
9. respect the deadlines they are given.				
10. solve problems on their own.				
11. adapt to new situations and new people.				
12. attain a goal by different means and with diverse solutions.				
13. anticipate problems rather than wait for things to happen.				

	Yes	Sometimes	No	Does not apply
14. use effective teaching strategies that lead to improved learning and achievement.				
15. establish rules and define them realistically.				
16. take risks.				
17. consider themselves as a front-row player when it comes to student achievement.				
18. self-motivate and self-support.				
Others:				

Table 4.8.   Self-Evaluation: Know Each Supervised Teacher Personally: Commitment and Motivation (adapted from Girard, McLean, & Morissette, 1992)

	Yes	Sometimes	No	Does not apply
My supervised teacher shows . . .				
1. their willingness to take on the responsibilities of a given task.				
2. their desire to develop professionally.				
3. their willingness to participate in a project (in this case teacher supervision) regardless of the tasks involved.				
4. their tenacity (the firm intention to see things through).				
5. their interest in taking the initiative (search for new practices) and their drive.				
6. their willingness to make decisions.				
7. their autonomy regarding the task at hand.				
8. their desire for flexibility and welcoming change.				
Others:				

What actions should I undertake to know more about the personal and profes-sional profile of my supervised teachers?

4.2.3—Know My Leadership and Management Styles

What the Supervisors Say

Many successful supervisors in our study described their leadership style as being far from authoritative:

- "I'm an easily approachable person. I am not authoritative. I love working in col-laboration, in consultation with people. I am not someone who imposes things. I love deciding things together, making decisions together. That's my profile." (Prin-cipal, Elementary)

Others revealed that the choice of leadership style was not their initiative and that their combination of pedagogical and transformational leadership style was born of necessity:

- "We have no other choice; we must use a participative style based on true con-sultation and pedagogical and transformational types of leadership." (Principal, Elementary)

How far do these testimonials reflect your experiences? (See Table 4.9.)

Table 4.9.   Self-Evaluation: Know My Leadership and Management Styles

	Yes	Sometimes	No	Does not apply
Directive management				
1. I focus my teacher supervision exclusively on evaluating my staff.				
2. I lead using directives, procedures, and rules.				
Others:				
Consultative management				
3. I make decisions after having consulted the persons involved.				

	Yes	Sometimes	No	Does not apply
4. I apply the consultation measures stipulated in the collective agreements.				
Others:				
Participative management				
5. I make a decision after having tried to obtain a consensus with the persons involved.				
6. I make a decision with all of the persons involved.				
Others:				
Situational leadership				
7. I consider the members' characteristics.				
8. I consider their level of development.				
9. I ask my teachers to make adjustments depending on the student results obtained at each reporting period.				
10. I look for a solution adapted to the situation and persons involved.				
Others:				
Transactional leadership				
11. I look for a win-win solution.				
12. I negotiate agreements between different teachers.				
13. I act as mediator when disputes arise.				
Others:				
Relational leadership				
14. I encourage discussion, and I participate in discussions with my staff.				
15. I congratulate the teacher for their project/efforts.				

(Continued)

Table 4.9. *(Continued)*

	Yes	Sometimes	No	Does not apply
16. I establish information and communication channels with my staff, the parents, and the students.				
17. I show a good mood when I go into the staff lounge.				
18. I use humor to relax the atmosphere, if necessary.				
19. I show empathy for the aspects that affect the personal lives of my supervised teachers.				
Others:				
Transformational leadership				
20. I provide my teachers with professional development opportunities that correspond to their needs.				
21. I celebrate the successes of my teachers and acknowledge their setbacks.				
22. I encourage my supervised teachers to do better by addressing their professional interests.				
Others:				
Pedagogical leadership				
23. I facilitate meetings on pedagogical practices.				
24. I make my pedagogical orientations known.				
25. I supervise and evaluate the effectiveness of my teachers' practices regarding student achievement.				
26. I learn to master the important elements of the education programs.				
27. I learn to master winning pedagogical practices.				
28. I lead PLCs on issues related to my school's priorities.				
Others:				

	Yes	Sometimes	No	Does not apply
Ethical leadership				
29. My decision is consistent with my educational values.				
30. My decision takes into account the good of the students.				
31. I act as the defender and the representative of my school with all of the stakeholders.				
32. I ensure confidentiality.				
Others:				
Shared leadership				
33. I delegate supervision duties to my vice principal(s).				
34. I promote collaboration between teachers to ensure the sharing of expertise.				
35. I recognize the potential of the teacher leaders.				
Others:				
Collaborative leadership				
36. I develop strategic actions with my school-team.				
37. I share the implementation of these strategic measures with my school-team.				
38. I involve the different staff members in these strategic actions.				
39. I use the expertise of the members of my school-team.				
Others:				

What actions should I undertake to improve my leadership and management styles?

See Table 4.10 for an exercise on leadership styles.

Table 4.10. Exercise—Supervisor's Leadership Styles

	Pedagogical	Relational	Transformational	Situational	Ethical	Shared	Collaborative
The following items pertain to leadership styles (pedagogical, relational, transformational, situational, ethical, shared, and collaborative). Choose the leadership style that correlates the most with each item (1 answer). Note: Leadership styles may apply to more than 1 item.							
1. I celebrate my school's successes, and I encourage my teachers to excel.							
2. I act as a defender and a representative of my school with all of the stakeholders.							
3. I supervise and evaluate the effectiveness of my school's teaching practices with regard to student achievement.							
4. I learn to master the important elements of education programs and the methods to assess student learning.							
5. I establish information and communication channels with my staff and my students.							
6. I delegate certain tasks to my vice principal or to the members of a work committee to help them learn.							
7. I encourage, recognize, and reward my teachers' and students' efforts and guide them to do better.							
8. I always appear to be in a good mood, and I often drop into the staff lounge.							
9. After each reporting period, I ask my teachers to make adjustments in light of the students' outcomes.							
10. I ensure confidentiality.							
11. I am always looking for win-win solutions.							
12. I serve as facilitator in PLCs on issues related to my school's priorities.							
13. I encourage my supervised teachers to do better by addressing their professional interests.							
14. I often use humor to relax the atmosphere when there is tension in the air.							

	Pedagogical	Relational	Transformational	Situational	Ethical	Shared	Collaborative
15. I am sensitive to aspects that affect the personal lives of my staff.							
16. I get groups to work together and support each other.							

Answers:

Pedagogical: 3, 4, 12

Relational: 5, 8, 14, 15

Transformational: 1, 3, 7, 13

Situational: 9, 11

Ethical: 2, 10

Shared: 6

Collaborative: 16

If you scored:
- 12 to 16 right answers, you know leadership styles very well.
- 7 to 11 right answers, you know leadership styles quite well.
- less than 7 right answers, your knowledge of leadership styles is limited. We encourage you to seek training in this regard.

4.2.4—Know the Services Provided by Human Resources to Support My Teacher Supervision Practice

What the Supervisors Say

Successful supervisors use human resources' expertise to deal with difficult teachers and to find and interpret relevant articles in the collective agreements.

- "To perform my supervision with difficult teachers or those having difficulties, I refer to my district's Human Resources and I am very satisfied with it." (Principal, Elementary)

- "Rather than search through the entire collective agreement to locate a particular article, I contact Human Resources who immediately finds it, and what's more, they interpret it for me." (Principal, Elementary)

- "I am not a lawyer so I don't try to interpret the articles in the collective agreements. I refer to my Human Resources Services." (Principal, Secondary)

How far do these testimonials reflect your experiences? (See Table 4.11.)

Table 4.11. Self-Evaluation: Know the Services Provided by Human Resources to Support My Teacher Supervision Practice

	Yes	Sometimes	No	Does not apply
I possess the knowledge/information provided by my district's Human Resources with regard to . . .				
1. the evaluation of nontenured faculty.				
2. the evaluation of teachers in a problem situation.				
3. the interpretation of collective agreements.				
As for me . . .				
4. I inform them of any problem situation pertaining to personnel management.				
Others:				

What actions should I undertake to better understand the services provided by Human Resources to support my teacher supervision practice?

4.2.5—Know Facilitation Techniques

What the Supervisors Say

Successful supervisors use certain specific facilitation techniques when performing teacher supervision with a group.

- "My role as pedagogical leader is also to be a facilitator with my teachers, whether in small or large groups." (Principal, Secondary)

- "To be the facilitator of a PLC or a work group, you have to know certain facilitation techniques: be clear in explaining the objectives of the meeting, get everyone to have a say, go around the table, use humor when needed, review and synthesize, etc." (Principal, Elementary)

How far do these testimonials reflect your experiences? (See Table 4.12.)

Table 4.12.   Self-Evaluation: Know Facilitation Techniques

	Yes	Sometimes	No	Does not apply
During group meetings . . .				
1. I listen.				
2. I reformulate what is being said.				
3. When I do not understand what is being said, I ask for clarification.				
4. I acknowledge the success stories.				
5. I ask my members to express their opinion on a given issue before I express my own opinion.				
6. I take emotions into account.				
7. I know how to find balance between work content and work climate.				
8. I make sure everyone has a say.				
Others:				

What actions should I undertake to better understand facilitation techniques?

Table 4.13 presents an overview of the most significant knowledge in supervision. *Can you think of any other pedagogical or human-resource-related knowledge?*

Table 4.13.   Synthesis of the Main Knowledge for Effective Supervision

Pedagogical Skills	*Human Relations Skills*
4.1.1 Have a pedagogical vision and educational values.	4.2.1 Know the organizational culture and particularities of my work environment.
4.1.2 Know the national and local policies pertaining to teacher supervision.	4.2.2 Know the personal and professional profile of each supervised teacher.
4.1.3 Know my school's issues regarding student achievement.	4.2.3 Know my leadership and management styles.
4.1.4 Know the resources provided by Education Services to support my teacher supervision practice.	4.2.4 Know the services provided by Human Resources to support my teacher supervision practice.
4.1.5 Know the basic principles of pedagogical supervision.	4.2.5 Know facilitation techniques.

Chapter Five

The *Know How to Do* Every Supervisor Should Possess

Knowing how to do refers to the skills that are necessary to perform a given task.

5.1—PEDAGOGICAL *KNOW HOW TO DO*

In this section, 12 pedagogical *know how to do*s pertaining to the orders of leadership (3), method (7), and cooperation (2) are examined.

- Use pedagogical leadership: Promote my vision of the school system, my educational orientations and values; encourage the professional development of my staff; support pedagogical projects and innovations.
- Use situational leadership: Focus on the students' needs and the school's education priorities.
- Manage ethnocultural diversity in my school.
- Organize my time to make teacher supervision a priority.
- Supervise the attainment of the achievement objectives.
- Encourage and support the pedagogical projects of my teachers and assist them in their professional development related to the school's priorities and the students' needs.
- Supervise the compliance to national/local policies and those of the school in matters of pedagogy.
- Financially support my teachers' pedagogical projects and professional development needs.
- Structure organization to enable teachers to attend professional development activities.
- Perform teacher supervision with no subjectivity.
- Establish work groups/PLCs in my school and encourage peer collaboration.
- Assist my school-team in finding and applying the most effective educational practices for the specific needs of the students.

Pedagogical Leadership

5.1.1—Use Pedagogical Leadership: Promote My Vision of the School System, My Educational Orientations and Values; Encourage the Pedagogical Development of My Staff; Support Pedagogical Projects and Innovations

What the Supervisors Say

Successful supervisors are molded by a strong pedagogical identity because of the fact that they were once teachers and have over the years distinguished themselves by their pedagogical vision and vitality:

- "We are first and foremost pedagogues because we were once teachers. If we have been chosen to be principal, it's because we've demonstrated pedagogical leadership here." (Principal, Elementary)

This strong identity is reflected when these supervisors speak of their practice:

- "When we have a supervision meeting, I find that it brings good energy. It's a leadership action, which is why it is important to make supervision a priority. When we call a parent, we do it because it's urgent. . . . After the supervision meeting, you feel you are in a position of leader. Here, I'm actually doing my job!" (Principal, Elementary)

Before launching new projects in their school, these pedagogical leaders must first look at their teachers' initiatives and then propose motivational directions or projects:

- "I do everything I can to support my teachers' proposals; otherwise, I suggest projects I hope will interest them." (Principal, Elementary)

Successful supervisors know the importance of attributing a more formal format to the supervision, with planning that extends over several years:

- "My goal for the next year is to organize common supervision missions . . . and planning. Over two or three years, what should we work on? . . . Getting organized in that sense. I think that it will have a direct impact on both student development and achievement." (Principal, Secondary)

How far do these testimonials reflect your experiences? (See Table 5.1.)

Table 5.1. Self-Evaluation: Use Pedagogical Leadership

	Yes	Sometimes	No	Does not apply
1. I promote my vision of pedagogical supervision.				
2. I encourage the professional development of my staff.				
3. I support pedagogical projects.				
4. I encourage pedagogical initiatives and innovation.				
5. I welcome new pedagogical methods.				
6. I encourage complementarity in pedagogical practices.				
7. I guide my team to develop a common vision with regard to the school's pedagogical orientations.				
Others:				

What actions should I undertake to develop my pedagogical leadership?

5.1.2—Use Situational Leadership: Focus on the Students' Needs and the School's Education Priorities

What the Supervisors Say

The successful supervisors in our study understood the impact of adequately meeting the inherent needs of their work context:

- "Our most important clients are the students, with all of their strengths and weaknesses. You have to listen to them, help them, and meet their needs, whether they are gifted students, those who excel, those who are average, or those with difficulties." (Principal, Elementary)

In other words, the supervisor's actions must center on the student, and their achievement must remain at all times their main focus:

- "Our priority as principal must be the student. Their success. If it's our own success as principal, we're in trouble." (Principal, Elementary)

Indeed, this adaptation can be particularly difficult in schools characterized by a significant heterogeneity:

- "My goal is to focus on the students who need resources . . . reexamine the students who need a revised intervention plan versus those who only need an action plan with their advisor. . . . You have to prioritize the right students. In Cycle 1, out of 125 students, I have around 70 intervention plans. If I would have had to revise all of these plans, it would have taken a lot of time. So we prioritized those students who were most in need. More resources are coming in April. I'm talking about refresher courses, additional recuperation measures for the students. I'm satisfied." (Vice Principal, Secondary)

It's important that in each school teachers contribute to the attainment of objectives:

- "Everyone in the school must be hands on if we are to reach the objectives of our educational priorities; it's everyone's business." (Principal, Vocational training)

How far do these testimonials reflect your experiences? (See Table 5.2.)

Table 5.2.   Self-Evaluation: Use Situational Leadership

	Yes	Sometimes	No	Does not apply
1. I provide services adapted to the students' needs.				
2. I am sensitive to the climate around me in my interventions.				
3. I adapt my interventions to the teacher's specific needs and characteristics.				
4. I take into account the data generated by the social, economic, and political context of my environment.				
5. I use the strengths of my teaching and nonteaching staff to solve a problem.				
6. I use the strengths of each of my teams to solve a problem.				
Others:				

What actions should I undertake to develop my situational leadership?

5.1.3 — *Manage Ethnocultural Diversity in My School*

🗩 *What the Supervisors Say*

The following statements were taken from interviews conducted with secondary- and elementary-level teacher supervisors from three Québec school districts as part of a research project titled "Pratiques exemplaires pour une meilleure inclusion des élèves immigrants dans les écoles" ("Exemplary Practices for a Greater Inclusion of Immigrant Students"), led by Professor Bouchamma and funded by the Québec Ministry of Education.

To implement the most effective educational practices to meet the school, social, and linguistic needs of immigrant students, these successful supervisors established preparatory classes and other measures to facilitate language learning:

- "The preparatory class in elementary school, where the student orally learns [the host language] is tremendously helpful for their integration into the [regular] classroom. Also, in cases there the student has been denied their basic rights or has experienced difficult or traumatizing situations, this class appears to be a more reassuring transitional phase." (Principal, Elementary)

Other supervisors drew attention to and supported the different cultures present in their school in other ways and encouraged their teams to do the same:

- "Every month, during our student assembly in the gymnasium, one country was represented and each immigrant student showed us their country's customs." (Principal, Elementary)

- "Every day during our Intercultural week, one country is highlighted and we learn about the different national anthems, flags, dances, food, etc." (Principal, Elementary)

Moreover, these supervisors encouraged their teachers to adjust their practices and evaluation mechanisms to better meet the needs of these new arrivals, to demonstrate openness, and to reflect on changing their perceptions of these new students:

- "Sometimes, all it takes is a little adapting to make things easier. I believe that having this open-mindedness makes it possible to move forward, one step and a time." (Principal, Secondary)

- "It makes you react, but do you know what you believe, do you know your own convictions? From that moment on, you have to give this person the space they need to discover that they can also choose their convictions. . . . You have to get them to look beyond the initial reaction." (Principal, Secondary)

How far do these testimonials reflect your experiences? (See Table 5.3.)

✓ Table 5.3. Self-Evaluation: Manage Ethnocultural Diversity in My School

	Yes	Sometimes	No	Does not apply
1. I allocate time for my teachers to discuss and get training on issues related to diversity management.				
2. I see to it that a community-school liaison agent is available for my teachers.				
3. I provide my school-team with information regarding the culture of immigrant students.				
4. I provide the families of immigrant students with information on the culture of the host society.				
5. I set up preparatory classes as well as measures for language teaching and learning.				
6. I integrate the immigrant students within the social and cultural life of the school (and I encourage my staff members to follow suit).				
7. I draw awareness to and support the different cultures present in my school (and I encourage my staff members to follow suit).				
Others:				

What actions should I undertake to manage ethnocultural diversity more effectively in my school?

Method

5.1.4—Organize My Time to Make Teacher Supervision a Priority

What the Supervisors Say

Supervisors consider supervision to be an indispensable activity that should not be ignored due to a lack of time:

- "You can't say you don't have the time. We're talking about an investment. So it's not true. I'm the first one to say that I don't have the time to work out, to go for a run. . . . [Supervision], it's a long-term investment. It's been proven." (Principal, Elementary)

- "It's sad that we don't make time for teacher supervision; we have so much work to do that supervision often goes to the bottom of the list, which is unfortunate." (Principal, Elementary)

Successful school leaders are aware of the importance of their pedagogical role, which often takes a back burner to their administrative duties. Prioritizing this role, delegating administrative tasks, and planning year-long supervision are excellent ways to turn things around:

- "If it's important, I have to make it a priority and put aside the administrative part of my job. I have to delegate." (Principal, Elementary)

- "For me, supervision is more a question of priority than of time. I have never done it, but this year, I plan my meetings in August. Once the school year has begun, priorities change. Teacher supervision has to be a priority but it is perceived as not being urgent. We always deal with the emergencies. So we push it back, push it back, we meet with teachers who are dealing with specific problems. So in August, you have to make time for it in the schedule." (Principal, Elementary)

- "I am capable of planning the meetings, even if I often lack the time. Better planning each step of my interventions, that's something I constantly work on." (Principal, Adult Education)

Effective supervisors see it as their responsibility to find solutions to the difficulty investing time in this process:

- "Part of the task is burdensome, but part of it is our responsibility. I humbly admit that there are moments when I feel I am losing control . . . but I quickly regain it and get it back." (Principal, Adult Education)

How far do these testimonials reflect your experiences? (See Table 5.4.)

Table 5.4. Self-Evaluation: Organize My Time to Make Teacher Supervision a Priority

	Yes	Sometimes	No	Does not apply
Teacher supervision is my priority. To have time to give it my full attention . . .				
1. I place it before my administrative duties.				
2. I plan my individual meetings at the beginning of the school year (and put it in my schedule).				
3. I plan my team meetings at the beginning of the school year.				
4. I delegate administrative duties to certain members of my staff (vice principal, teaching or nonteaching staff).				
5. I delegate certain pedagogical responsibilities to teacher leaders and ask them for reports.				

(Continued)

Table 5.4. *(Continued)*

	Yes	Sometimes	No	Does not apply
6. I keep informed on the PLC meetings I miss by reading the minutes or their written reports.				
7. I ask the mentors and sponsors (peers) to report on the supervision of some of their peers.				
8. I ask my teachers to build their professional portfolio, and I follow up.				
Others:				

What actions should I undertake to better organize my time to make teacher supervision a priority?

5.1.5—Supervise the Attainment of the Achievement Objectives

See Table 5.6 for an exercise on the supervision process.

What the Supervisors Say

The successful supervisor knows the importance of the school's orientations and state performance objectives and always ensures accountability:

- "I have to supervise the implementation of the education project, because it's my school's reality. Why? Because this is what continuously drives it. Reaching the objectives is important for each person involved." (Principal, Elementary)

- "I am accountable for this [our results] at the end of the school year and during my meetings with my superiors. You understand the importance." (Principal, Elementary)

How far do these testimonials reflect your experiences? (See Table 5.5.)

Table 5.5. Self-Evaluation: Supervise the Attainment of the Achievement Objectives

	Yes	*Sometimes*	*No*	*Does not apply*
1. My staff and I go over my objectives and actions at the end of each reporting period of the school year.				
2. I make the necessary adjustments to our actions during the year.				
3. Following my annual evaluation, I readjust my plan for the next year.				
4. I report on the results obtained in regard to the established objectives.				
Others:				

Table 5.6. Exercise—My Teacher Supervision Process

Name of the school: _____

Subject of the supervision: _____

Objective: _____

Type of supervision: ☐ individual   ☐ collective   ☐ individual and collective

Actions regarding the objective	Dates	Supervision Activities	Individual supervision	Collective supervision	Dates	Persons in charge	Measures to evaluate the objective

5.1.6—Encourage and Support the Pedagogical Projects of My Teachers and Assist Them in Their Professional Development Related to the School's Priorities and the Students' Needs

What the Supervisors Say

Effective supervisors possess the necessary resources to support their teachers' projects, which may address different needs, namely, financial, material, or human resources:

- "As principal, I must do everything in my power to support my staff, whether it be human resources or financial ones. I must be organized enough to say yes to their projects." (Principal, Elementary)

These requests for support must be consistent with the school's education priorities:

- "All of the requests for support and professional development must be based on the school's priorities. The first question I ask them is 'How does your project fit in with our school's priorities?'" (Principal, Elementary)

In some schools, this support may translate to something more structured or formal, such as a group of peers to evaluate proposed projects and make recommendations:

- "I set up a pedagogical innovation committee in my school and I gave them funds to help them take on a few projects and support them during the year." (Principal, Elementary)

- "When a government representative or a university proposes a pedagogical innovation project to me, I immediately ask some of my teachers to get involved." (Principal, Secondary)

- "I don't want to give them training . . . and let it stop there. If I really want practices to change in my school, I have to guide my staff all the way; I must go over what we've learned from time to time; that's what teacher supervision is all about." (Principal, Elementary)

Far too often, supervisors don't have the time to ensure a follow-up once the training is over. It is important to schedule these follow-ups to go over the training and acquired knowledge together:

- "It's interesting to see what they [the teachers] do, for example, during their training. I don't always have the time to check on them after their training, how it went. You always have to mark these reminders down in your schedule to do the follow-ups." (Principal, Secondary)

How far do these testimonials reflect your experiences? (See Table 5.7.)

Table 5.7. Self-Evaluation: Encourage and Support the Pedagogical Projects of My Teachers and Assist Them in Their Professional Development Related to the School's Priorities and the Students' Needs

	Yes	Sometimes	No	Does not apply
1. I make material and financial resources available for my teachers.				
2. I meet one-on-one with my pedagogical leaders to generate new projects.				
3. I periodically meet with my teachers who have undertaken a project.				
4. I encourage teachers who have undertaken a project to continuously evaluate their progress.				
5. I encourage teachers who have undertaken a project to make their winning practices known.				
Others:				

What actions should I undertake to develop, encourage, and support the pedagogical projects of my teachers?

5.1.7—Supervise the Compliance to National/Local Policies and Those of the School in Matters of Pedagogy

What the Supervisors Say

One successful supervisor in our study made an extensive list containing all of the policies so as to systematically verify their application:

- "I drew up a list of the elements of national and local [school districts] . . . and those of my school to check how these are being implemented." (Principal, Elementary)

Because it is the cycle team who is closely involved in the elaboration of the action plan, decisions are shared among the members responsible for its implementation and progress:

- "(Our academic success plan) is a document done by the Cycle-team and not by me, which explains the shared decisions and the fact that they are the ones responsible . . . for its application and sustainment." (Principal, Elementary)

Education services include instruction services, as well as complementary and specific services for the students:

- "My multidisciplinary committee is composed of learning specialists, psychologists, and other specialists. This committee agreed to prioritize which services should be provided to the students." (Principal, Elementary)

It is a question not only of organizing services but also of ensuring supervision and follow-up during the various stages of the process. It is the supervisor's responsibility to see that things go well and to make adjustments when necessary:

- "At each reporting period of the year—and not only at the beginning of the year—I check with my team to see if it's necessary, if at all possible, to make changes in my organization." (Principal, Elementary)

Supervisors focus their pedagogical supervision on the education programs, existing teaching strategies, and teaching practices:

- "In my individual and collective supervision, I emphasize the importance of respecting the education programs, because our students are evaluated on that." (Principal, Elementary)

The availability of resources does not necessarily mean that they are used. Indeed, some teachers simply refuse to be subjected to the proposed aid (they can accept or refuse), which can be a perplexing situation for some supervisors:

- "What do I do with those who refuse professional development, for different reasons? Do I force them, take disciplinary measures?" (Principal, Secondary)

To identify the teachers' needs, the effective supervisor uses tact, asks questions, encourages them, and may consider disciplinary measures as a last resort:

- "Being able to question the teacher face to face to obtain what we need, to question their practice, create a doubt. These are techniques that we principals have developed and use. In teacher supervision, it's just as important to question the teachers without them feeling judged. Just ask questions. I think it eventually brings them around without them feeling like they are being threatened." (Principal, Elementary)

Effective supervisors support their teachers during the implementation of reforms or the introduction of new practices, which can be challenging:

- "I set up a committee to supervise the implementation of a new teaching program and I launched a PLC to share the winning practices and challenges encountered during the implementation of this new program." (Principal, Elementary)

- "At this moment in my career, I've seen a lot of implementations of all sorts of things! I find that we don't pay enough attention to the time factor. We want the changes to occur rapidly, sometimes too rapidly." (Principal, Secondary)

When reforms are not adapted to the context and characteristics of the school in which they are being introduced, this can be an issue:

- "Take a high school that has 100 teachers; when you want to introduce something new, it's different from an elementary school where you have 15 teachers. Change can't always happen at the same speed. We always forget this. We find other reasons." (Principal, Secondary)

When introducing reforms, every good supervisor calls in reinforcement:

- "What helped us was that this proposed change came from the source. We tried to involve everyone concerned." (Vice Principal, Elementary)

However, when the objectives of a reform fail to address the concerns of the actors involved, the level of collaboration may be challenged:

- "It was not possible to consider the needs of each person. . . . We concentrated on one approach, we got everyone involved. We had established a work deadline. Generally speaking, it was about people . . . three individuals [who were opposed] against everyone else. You can't generalize." (Principal, Secondary)

Then there is the situation where everyone is on board but the lack of material resources compromises successful implementation:

- "We were introducing this new pedagogy, we were in it, but they had to continue without the proper pedagogical material." (Principal, Secondary)

How far do these testimonials reflect your experiences? (See Table 5.8.)

Table 5.8. Self-Evaluation: Supervise the Compliance to National/Local Policies and Those of the School in Matters of Pedagogy

	Yes	Sometimes	No	Does not apply
I supervise . . .				
1. the education services (teaching services, complementary and specific services) provided in my school.				
2. the application of education programs.				

(Continued)

Table 5.8. *(Continued)*

	Yes	Sometimes	No	Does not apply
3. the development of my teachers' skills.				
4. the implementation steps of a pedagogical reform.				
5. the application of national/local policies pertaining to pedagogy.				
6. my teachers' evaluative practices.				
In my approach to introduce change . . .				
7. I draw a portrait of the situation.				
8. I supervise the introduction of new practices.				
9. I supervise and evaluate the results of this change.				
10. I involve the staff who will be experiencing this reform.				
11. I provide them with the necessary resources (material, temporal, etc.).				
12. I establish one or more facilitating structures to accompany the reform (work groups, PLCs).				
13. I mobilize the persons involved toward common objectives in regard to the change to be introduced.				
Others:				

What actions should I undertake to supervise the compliance to national/local policies and those of the school in matters of pedagogy?

5.1.8—Financially Support My Teachers' Pedagogical Projects and Professional Development Needs

What the Supervisors Say

Supervisors are able to use small amounts of allocated funding for projects associated with their priorities and may actively seek out additional funding through collaborations with outside organizations to support new projects and develop the necessary activities to meet the students' needs.

- "Sometimes, it's good to turn to the district to get financial support for professional development. I can go get a few hundred dollars here and there, every little bit helps." (Principal, Elementary)

- "I give my people time off to participate in professional learning communities (PLCs). . . . Four or five meetings a year . . . How they feel when they arrive, when they are allowed to attend, I think it's very important. Volunteering, sure it's easier to participate when you are given the time off to do so." (Principal, Elementary)

- "The requests involved requests for time off to participate, book purchases . . . requests for literature or books to help us in science, in math." (Principal, Elementary)

How far do these testimonials reflect your experiences? (See Table 5.9.)

Table 5.9.   Self-Evaluation: Financially Support My Teachers' Pedagogical Projects and Professional Development Needs

	Yes	Sometimes	No	Does not apply
1. I provide financial resources to support my teachers' pedagogical projects, particularly if they pertain to our priorities.				
2. I submit funding requests to my school district services.				
3. I submit funding requests to my school's foundation.				
4. I use the amounts allotted for each teacher for their professional development, as laid out in their employee agreement.				
5. I ask local businesses to help finance our projects.				
6. I develop projects in partnership with universities to offer training programs for my teachers.				
Others:				

What actions should I undertake to financially support my teachers' pedagogical projects and professional development needs?

5.1.9—Structure Organization to Enable Teachers to Attend Professional Development Activities

What the Supervisors Say

An effective supervisor uses different strategies to enable teachers to attend pedagogical activities:

- "In August, when I prepare the teachers' schedule, I do everything I can to free the same periods for them so they can get together." (Principal, Secondary)

- "I use half-days [professional development days]. I organize meetings for them during available periods, I let them out of class. With all of these meetings, I have PLCs that work really well." (Principal, Elementary)

How far do these testimonials reflect your experiences? (See Table 5.10.)

Table 5.10.   Self-Evaluation: Structure Organization to Enable Teachers to Attend Professional Development Activities

	Yes	Sometimes	No	Does not apply
1. When planning the schedule, I schedule the same free periods for the members in my school-team/in the same department/in the same cycle to allow them to meet together.				
2. I take advantage of the means provided by my teachers' national/local employee agreements to facilitate their professional development.				
3. I make full use of the professional development days and monthly after-school meetings to hold pedagogical meetings.				
Others:				

What actions should I undertake to enable my teachers to attend professional development activities more often?

5.1.10—Perform Teacher Supervision With No Subjectivity

What the Supervisors Say

Successful supervisors grasp the implications of subjectivity in the supervision process:

- "When I have to do an evaluation at the end of a particular supervision, I have to avoid subjectivity as much as possible." (Principal, Elementary)

- "In supervision, it's always hard to be totally objective; even in the evaluation, there is always a small portion of subjectivity." (Vice Principal, Elementary)

To avoid possible biases, this supervisor shares a practice:

- "In my individual supervision interviews, I always start with data, facts, and observations to remove any subjectivity from my interventions." (Principal, Secondary)

How far do these testimonials reflect your experiences? (See Table 5.11.)

Table 5.11.   Self-Evaluation: Perform Teacher Supervision with No Subjectivity

	Yes	Sometimes	No	Does not apply
In my judgments . . .				
1. I consider the information confirming my beliefs as much as I do contradictory information (confirmation bias).				
2. I consider all of my supervised teachers' characteristics (halo effect).				
3. I avoid comparing my supervised teachers: I am aware that they are not all at the same stage of professional development (contrast effect).				
4. I avoid adopting ready-made opinions of certain individuals who have different sociodemographic characteristics (stereotype effect).				
5. I am able to be objective regarding how information is presented to me (framing error; e.g., information presented in terms of success or failure, the number of successes without considering the percentages, etc.).				
6. I am aware that the examples that come to mind cannot solely represent the situation at hand (remembered availability bias and representativeness).				
Others:				

What actions should I undertake to be more objective in my supervision?

Cooperation

5.1.11 — Establish Work Groups/PLCs in My School and Encourage Peer Collaboration

What the Supervisors Say

The needs analysis conducted by means of a questionnaire administered to teachers from two school districts involved in our research-action-training project revealed that they were highly motivated by collaborative work and in particular by their interest in sharing their teaching practices. In the interviews with their supervisors in this same study, the latter acknowledged their teachers' interest in collaborations, which in some cases took place on a volunteer basis:

- "It was the teachers who asked me to get together when they were available to discuss their practices. I was so proud of them." (Principal, Secondary)

- "PLCs start with the teachers." (Principal, Elementary).

When several teams are at work in the same school, exchange and discussion are encouraged, which in turn enables the supervisor to gather data for their supervision:

- "Each person presents what they do to the others. The results of the Cycle 1 team: Here is what we have accomplished, here are our successes, our issues, this is what we should do . . . to address these difficulties. . . . That's how my pedagogical supervision works." (Principal, Elementary)

Working in collaboration brings teachers to form a PLC:

- "We started with a lot of statistical data. . . . We started with observable behaviors and teacher surveys on evaluations. . . . Then together we shared the measures we should adopt. I believe that we had become a PLC." (Principal, Elementary)

In addition to the discussions between PLC members, these groups organized meetings with other groups:

- "The PLC is one method among others to conduct teacher supervision, but in a subgroup. The role of the supervisor is finding a balance in all of that. It's an integrative concept between [the legal considerations], the work groups, the leadership styles." (Vice Principal, Secondary)

- "We all talk to each other in the PLC, you have to be coherent in your actions, because the question rapidly arises." (Principal, Elementary)

The supervisor therefore takes on the role of pedagogical facilitator:

- "A PLC . . . it's above all a place where you can lead discussions on pedagogy, where you can encourage discussion between colleagues and the sharing of practices and experiences. Our role becomes more that of facilitator, of moderator. It becomes . . . a supervision tool in terms of the school's priorities." (Principal, Elementary)

- "In my role as principal, I listen, I know the teaching practices and I see the group evolving. I see the priorities evolving as well. All of these PLCs begin by looking at the students' outcomes." (Principal, Elementary)

Supervisors essentially structure their inception into a PLC, their work processes, the length of their meetings, their targeted objectives and themes, and their use of meeting minutes in subsequent meetings.

- "In our school, we've been PLCs for two years and we continue to do so. I meet with the group leaders early in the process. In the beginning, we ask ourselves a lot of questions. It's never more than two hours long during a PD [professional development] day, because when it's longer, we get distracted. There is a lot of progress and positive discussion. It always ends on what we are going to talk about at our next meeting. The focus is always pedagogy. There is always a report of each meeting. I receive this report. I attend one or the other meeting. I learn a lot from the minutes. It's not too hard, it's not a full half-day. I would like to do another one, between now and the end of the year. Slowly but surely, we get better. It's really something to create this. In the end, what matters is that we talk about pedagogy." (Principal, Secondary)

Effective supervisors are appreciated for their collaboration because their teachers share responsibilities with them regarding accountability. The power shared with teachers reassures them:

- "The PLC made us both responsible for accountability. Now, one of the teachers from the PLC is on the school council. I am no longer alone. It's wonderful. It's a healthier atmosphere in the school." (Principal, Elementary)

How far do these testimonials reflect your experiences? (See Table 5.12.)

Table 5.12.　Self-Evaluation: Establish Work Groups/PLCs in My School and Encourage Peer Collaboration

	Yes	Sometimes	No	Does not apply
To favor collaboration . . .				
1. I offer the necessary training.				
2. I speak of the benefits of collaboration.				
3. I make sure that material and financial resources are available for my work groups/PLC.				
4. I encourage collaborative work.				
5. I structure organization to favor collaboration by making the necessary changes (time, space, rules, and regulations).				

(Continued)

Table 5.12. *(Continued)*

	Yes	Sometimes	No	Does not apply
6. I consider my teachers to be experts in their field.				
7. I exercise shared and adapted leadership (transformational, socio-constructivist, etc.).				
8. I take advantage of opportunities to explain and reiterate my role in the PLC.				
9. I favor measurable objectives focused on student learning.				
10. I show gratitude.				
To favor collaboration, I guide my teachers/my team to . . .				
11. voluntarily join a collaborative team.				
12. identify a common vision, values, and objectives toward collective accountability for the student.				
13. refocus their pedagogical discussions on student achievement.				
14. adopt effective communication based on mutual respect and trust.				
15. take on shared responsibilities.				
16. be interdependent.				
17. contribute equitably.				
18. demonstrate a willingness to improve.				
19. promote teamwork.				
20. adopt an equal status within the group.				
21. use data to follow the students' progress.				
22. reflect on the impact of their pedagogical practices.				
Others:				

What actions should I undertake to establish work groups/PLCs in my school and encourage peer collaboration?

Table 5.13 provides a diagnostic tool to determine which stage of development your PLC is in. It is only relevant if you have one or more PLCs in your school. Answer these questions for each PLC. Indicate your level of agreement on each item.

Table 5.13. Exercise—My PLC Is at Which Stage of Development?

	Yes	Sometimes	No	Does not apply	*If Yes/Sometimes:* How is this noticeable? Provide an example. *If No:* Suggest actions.
1. As school leader and member of the PLC . . .					
1. I use my practice to demonstrate the connection between the priorities and the actions we undertake.					
2. I empower the teachers to make decisions regarding their students' needs.					
3. I take the opportunity to explain/reiterate my role within the PLC.					
4. I refocus pedagogical discussions toward student achievement.					
5. I favor measurable objectives focused on student learning.					
2. As members of the PLC, my teaching and nonteaching staff . . .					
6. have quality time for collaborative meetings.					
7. meet during work hours.					
8. are responsible for all of the students (*our* student rather than your/my student).					
9. understand their role.					
10. understand my role.					
11. influence each other.					
12. influence me.					
13. appreciate my presence.					
14. understand that the collaborative meetings improve their professional development as well as student learning.					
15. can manage themselves.					
16. transform what they share into collective learning.					
17. discuss issues related to learning.					

(Continued)

Table 5.13. *(Continued)*

	Yes	Sometimes	No	Does not apply	If Yes/Sometimes: How is this noticeable? Provide an example. If No: Suggest actions.
18. collectively solve problems and share their expertise.					
19. choose themes for discussion that are related to student learning issues.					
20. make sure that the themes discussed enable them to review actions undertaken between the meetings.					
21. consider the students' profile and growth in the planning and content of each meeting.					
22. consider the team's progress in the planning and content of each meeting.					
23. base their decisions on accurate data.					
3. The PLC members use data on a regular basis . . .					
24. to follow their students' progress.					
25. to perform complex analyses.					
26. to reflect on the impact of their pedagogical actions.					
4. The culture of collaboration within the PLC encourages . . .					
27. authentic dialogue (individuals can truly speak their mind).					
28. open-mindedness.					
29. healthy communication.					
30. a constructive critical mind.					
Based on your answers, give yourself 2 points for a *YES* and 1 point for a *SOMETIMES*.					
Number of *YES*es × 2					
Total:					
If your score is between *12 and 23*, your PLC is in its *initiation* stage, where collaborative work has begun. *24 and 46*, your PLC is in its *implementation* stage; it's going well, with a few aspects remaining to work on. *47 and 68*, your PLC is in its *integration* stage, the highest level of a community that reflects on and shares its professional practices and is invested in collaborative work.					

- If your answer is *yes* or *sometimes*, please explain how it is noticeable in your school and provide an example.
- If your answer is *no*, think about positive actions you could undertake in your school.

5.1.12 — Assist My School-Team in Finding and Applying the Most Effective Educational Practices for the Specific Needs of the Students

💬 What the Supervisors Say

A good supervisor uses pedagogical leadership by documenting their teachers on advances in the teaching field and by inviting speakers to their school for this purpose.

- "In my weekly information bulletin, I show my teachers the books, the relevant websites, the success stories going on in other schools. . . . I invite speakers for this purpose and I encourage experimentation." (Principal, Elementary)

During their supervision, an effective action is to direct their supervised teacher's attention toward those students for whom the teacher has not developed an intervention plan. Following each reporting period, the teacher is then asked to respond to questions on what measures they have taken with each of these students:

- "At the end of each reporting period, I present a grid to each of my teachers and I write down the names of the students who have not succeeded in reading, writing, and math, with their results. I then ask the teacher to tell me what they are currently doing to support these students in their learning. Do they see the learning specialist? Do they have an intervention plan? Does this student get help with their homework? Is this student monitored somehow? It helps me to better follow these students. So at the end of each reporting period, I compare the results with those of the first report card; I follow up like that, and at the end of the year, well I am so happy to see that student. We saved them. Yeh!" (Principal, Elementary)

The effective supervisor thus makes sure that each teacher understands that student achievement is the ultimate purpose of the supervision and that each teacher is accountable for their students' progress. When necessary, the supervisor may schedule a meeting to reconfirm priorities:

- "When we defined teacher supervision, we said that the ultimate goal was the success of our students. When someone does not responsibly invest in the PLC, this shows in the student's outcomes. For example, when a teacher fails to schedule reading routines, well, eventually, there is an impact. The student falls behind the following year. We can . . . identify [which teacher] the student was with. Along the way, it's bad for our students. We want to encourage student success. It's our responsibility to meet with these teachers, to get them to understand that they [are not] alone [in the school]. When we clearly establish things that way, it has an impact." (Principal, Elementary)

How far do these testimonials reflect your experiences? (See Table 5.14.)

Table 5.14. Self-Evaluation: Assist My School-Team in Finding and Applying the Most Effective Educational Practices for the Specific Needs of the Students

	Yes	Sometimes	No	Does not apply
To adopt and encourage new educational practices . . .				
1. I go into the classrooms to encourage the students and teachers who undertake new projects.				
2. I inform my teachers on advances in the field.				
3. I encourage my teachers to go into other classes/other schools.				
4. I encourage my teachers to experiment with new didactic materials and teaching practices.				
Others:				

5.2—*KNOW HOW TO DO* IN HUMAN RELATIONS

In this section, we have retained 18 *know how to do*s in human relations pertaining to transversal leadership skills (4), methodology (6), cooperation (1), communication (1), and ethics (6).

- Use relational leadership: Encourage communication, consultation, and discussion among the teachers.
- Use transformational leadership: Inspire, stimulate, optimize the potential of each teacher, and empower them toward self-reliance.
- Delegate support duties and responsibilities to the vice principal and to teachers and closely monitor.
- Maintain staff awareness of the main orientations and general objectives regarding student achievement.
- Objectively analyze the school's climate.
- Develop and implement a pluriannual supervision plan for my teachers.
- Use data collection and analysis tools.
- Agree to the mutual expectations during the individual/group supervision process.
- Guide each supervised teacher to self-evaluate and set professional growth objectives.
- Provide constructive individual/group feedback following supervision activities and follow up accordingly.
- Consult school district services for specific expertise.
- Communicate clearly with my teachers.

- Encourage and organize development activities based on the school's needs and those of the teachers.
- Use differentiated supervision for behaviors related to the motivation, commitment, and professional competence of the supervised teacher.
- Ensure that the rules of confidentiality are respected.
- Acknowledge the personal/collective contributions and successes of my teachers.
- Demonstrate managerial courage in certain supervision situations.
- Declare my intentions and explain my supervision actions.

Leadership

You can use Table 5.15 to evaluate if you have what it takes to be a good leader. To begin this reflection, we invite you to evaluate these components of your leadership using a rating between 1 (very little) and 5 (a lot) for each quality, with 5 being the highest rating.

Table 5.15. Exercise—Do You Have What It Takes to Be a Leader? (Samson, 2008)

	My evaluation				
	1	*2*	*3*	*4*	*5*
I possess the following qualities:					
1. I am open-minded toward others.					
2. I am a good listener for my teachers.					
3. I have a positive view of my teachers.					
4. I have the desire to see others succeed.					
5. I have the desire to learn professionally.					
6. I want to share my knowledge with my teachers and my colleagues.					
7. I am capable of making the right decisions.					
8. I have a positive attitude toward difficulties.					
9. I am capable of performing disciplinary measures when necessary.					
10. I demonstrate a certain amount of sacrifice, of selflessness, in my role as principal.					
11. I have a systemic vision of my school.					
Total:					

If you have scored:

- *50 to 55,* you have evaluated yourself to be an excellent leader.
- *44 to 49,* you have evaluated yourself to be a very good leader.
- *35 to 43,* you have evaluated yourself to be an average leader.
- *less than 35,* there is still work to do and this experience will hopefully help!

5.2.1—Use Relational Leadership: Encourage Communication, Consultation, and Discussion Among the Teachers

☐ *What the Supervisors Say*

A good supervisor knows how to analyze their relationships with their supervised teachers and evaluate their relational leadership skills:

- "The entire supervision is relational: my relationships with the staff are good, my social relations are excellent, I communicate often, I go into the classrooms with the teacher's consent, our discussions are numerous and fruitful. I am proud of my team and also proud of myself. I think I have good public relations skills." (Principal, Elementary)

- "I demonstrate a welcoming attitude. I make my supervised teacher comfortable during our meetings. Good human relations helps the supervision process." (Principal, Elementary)

How far do these testimonials reflect your experiences? (See Table 5.16.)

✓ **Table 5.16. Self-Evaluation: Use Relational Leadership: Encourage Communication, Consultation, and Discussion Among the Teachers**

	Yes	Sometimes	No	Does not apply
1. I establish communication networks with my entire school-team.				
2. I encourage debate and the exchange of ideas on pedagogical issues.				
3. I participate with my teachers in shared practice groups.				
4. I know the profile of each person I supervise.				
5. I prefer a humanistic approach in my relationships with my staff rather than a hierarchical approach.				
6. I participate as much as I can in the social activities organized in my school.				
7. I have a jovial nature.				
Others:				

What actions should I undertake to improve my relational leadership?

Table 5.17 contains an exercise that will help you evaluate the quality of your relationship with your staff. The more you answered *no* to these questions, the more you should review some of your attitudes with your employees. If you did not know what to answer to any of the questions, consider your answer to be *no*. In your opinion, what attitudes should you work on?

Table 5.17.   Exercise—The Quality of My Relationship with My Staff (adapted from Publications du Québec, 1994)

When I have a relationship with the members of my school-team . . .	*Yes*	*Sometimes*	*No*	*Does not apply*
1. I trust them.				
2. I am calm and relaxed with them.				
3. I enjoy being in their company.				
4. I am concerned about how they are doing personally.				
5. I am concerned about how they are doing professionally.				
6. I am concerned for their well-being.				
7. I am welcoming and friendly.				
8. I can admit my errors to them.				
9. I am able to express the appreciation or criticism they deserve.				
10. I want to help them in their career and professional growth.				
11. I can be discreet and a good confidant.				
12. I can confront them with assurance.				
13. I can be tolerant with them, depending on the situation.				
14. I can communicate good news to them as much as I can bad news.				
15. I am ready to defend them when I share their point of view.				
16. I give them the help they need to advance.				

5.2.2 — Use Transformational Leadership: Inspire, Stimulate, Optimize the Potential of Each Teacher, and Empower Them Toward Self-Reliance

🗨 *What the Supervisors Say*

Successful supervisors are well versed in winning practices and particularly the strong attributes of each teacher when introducing change:

- "In each supervised teacher, I identify the aspects that drive them and I provide them with growth opportunities in the areas that motivate them the most." (Principal, Elementary)

- "I maximize the strengths of my supervised teachers and I show them my appreciation." (Principal, Secondary)

- "In the PLCs I had this year, I have a teacher who demonstrates good pedagogical leadership, who is also recognized by their peers. I will use this person a lot as a pillar to support the establishment of other learning communities." (Principal, Vocational)

How far do these testimonials reflect your experiences? (See Table 5.18.)

Table 5.18. Self-Evaluation: Use Transformational Leadership: Inspire, Stimulate, Optimize the Potential of Each Teacher, and Empower Them Toward Self-Reliance

	Yes	Sometimes	No	Does not apply
1. I help my teachers to better understand the school's objectives and orientations and to own them.				
2. I instill in them pride, respect, trust, and the conviction of accomplishing the school's mission.				
3. I encourage my teachers to look beyond their personal interests to consider those of others.				
4. I use collective intellectual stimulation.				
5. I encourage my teachers to be rational and rigorous when solving problems.				
6. I recognize individual contributions.				
7. I pay attention to each person and treat each one as being unique.				
8. I contribute to increasing my teachers' motivation by considering their interests.				
9. I give them tasks to develop new skills.				

	Yes	Sometimes	No	Does not apply
10. I encourage teamwork.				
11. I identify and emphasize the strengths of my teachers.				
12. I use constructive feedback.				
13. I welcome creativity.				
14. I empower my supervised teachers.				
15. My actions optimize the potential of the members of my school-team.				
16. I stimulate their growth by setting high but realistic expectations.				
Others:				

What actions should I undertake to develop my transformational leadership?

5.2.3 — Delegate Support Duties and Responsibilities to the Vice Principal and to Teachers and Closely Monitor

What the Supervisors Say

A principal participating in our study who did not have a vice principal found it difficult to delegate:

- "It's not easy talking about delegating when you are responsible for two schools and you don't have a vice principal to work with!" (Principal, Elementary)

In contrast, a vice principal wished that they were given greater teacher supervision responsibilities:

- "When an observation is proposed with a teacher, we are told that, as vice principal, it's not our job. We have to go through that. We have to help our teachers to grow. The principal can delegate and the vice principal can have among their duties, for example, the supervision of certain teachers and certain priorities." (Vice Principal, Secondary)

Other school leaders felt that certain supervision duties could be delegated to teacher-leaders:

- "In my school, I have some great pedagogical leaders who inspire others a lot. I can therefore delegate certain tasks to them." (Principal, Elementary)

How far do these testimonials reflect your experiences? (See Table 5.19.)

Table 5.19. Self-Evaluation: Delegate Support Duties and Responsibilities to the Vice Principal and to Teachers and Closely Monitor

	Yes	Sometimes	No	Does not apply
1. I am capable of delegating certain support tasks to my vice principal or to teachers.				
2. We come to an agreement as to which approach to use.				
3. I remain informed regarding the delegated tasks through an activity report submitted at different times during the year.				
4. I follow up with the person to whom I have delegated a responsibility related to supervision.				
5. I trust them.				
Others:				

What actions should I undertake to increase my delegation of support tasks and responsibilities to my vice principal and my teachers?

5.2.4—Maintain Staff Awareness of the Main Orientations and General Objectives Regarding Student Achievement

What the Supervisors Say

Effective supervisors work with their school-team to identify objectives, determine strategies, develop practices, and ensure feedback and follow-up.

- "[First], we developed our first action plan with SMART objectives. We set a goal to increase by 3% our achievement in reading. So we started reflecting on this together, started analyzing what was already in place.' What are we doing at this moment? We must be doing something right if reading achievement is at 90%! So in the beginning, we don't throw everything out the window. No. We look at what works. The students who are not performing, what do they need? . . . So these different strategies we reflected on together are in the action plan. And that's where accountability comes in. For example: Did you change our schedule to make sure that these three students get the support they need?" (Principal, Elementary)

The teaching and nonteaching staff all work together on reaching the goals laid out in the action plan. In a sense, by identifying actions to undertake, the staff assimilates this plan, which then becomes a source of motivation:

- "We spent a full PD day trying to find the most effective actions to implement to reach the objectives in our action plan. They were all highly motivated to do this work which they felt was a very practical thing to do." (Principal, Elementary)

Mobilization is also invaluable in accountability processes. In this case, the *we, our,* and *ours* support the weight the school places on this action plan, and the entire staff is involved in the process from day 1:

- "Consistency in our actions, gestures, and measures, and above all the commitment of the entire staff is necessary right from the start of the elaboration of the work plan. I'm talking about *our* plan, about *our* students, about *our* school. We determined [the foundations] together." (Principal, Elementary)

How far do these testimonials reflect your experiences? (See Table 5.20.)

Table 5.20. Self-Evaluation: Maintain Staff Awareness of the Main Orientations and General Objectives Regarding Student Achievement

	Yes	Sometimes	No	Does not apply
To mobilize my supervised teachers, I get them involved in . . .				
1. the development of the action plan.				
2. work groups and PLCs.				
I take advantage of different opportunities to . . .				
3. remind them of the school's orientations.				
4. request that they adopt the school's orientations and values.				
5. get them involved in the development of action plans.				
I promote, encourage, and reward . . .				
6. their sense of pride regarding their practice.				
7. their efforts when they go beyond expectations.				
8. the effectiveness of their teaching.				
9. their tangible collaboration.				
10. their contribution to the climate in terms of the work relations within the school.				
11. their presence and their stability.				
12. their concerns relative to student achievement.				
13. their sense of belonging to their school.				
Others:				

What actions should I undertake to increase staff awareness of the main orienta-tions and general objectives regarding student achievement?

Table 5.21 contains an exercise you can use to evaluate the mobilization of your staff.

Table 5.21.   Exercise—Evaluate the Mobilization of My Staff *(adapted from the journal CENTRACCÈS PME, 1995)*

The following statements serve to evaluate the level of mobilization in your school.

1. If you were to rate the level of staff mobilization on a scale from 1 to 10, what would be your spontaneous answer?

Demobilized   1   2   3   4   5   6   7   8   9   10   Mobilized

2. Identify tangible mobilization/demobilization factors within your school.

Mobilizing Factors	Demobilizing Factors

3. Specifically, staff mobilization can be measured by several indicators. Rate them for your school's staff, with _10_ being the highest rating.

They comply with the school's orientations:	1 2 3 4 5 6 7 8 9 10
They are involved in developing the annual action plan:	1 2 3 4 5 6 7 8 9 10
They have a sense of pride regarding teaching:	1 2 3 4 5 6 7 8 9 10
They make efforts beyond expectations:	1 2 3 4 5 6 7 8 9 10
They are effective in their duties:	1 2 3 4 5 6 7 8 9 10
They collaborate with peers/with the principal:	1 2 3 4 5 6 7 8 9 10
They have good work relations with the principal:	1 2 3 4 5 6 7 8 9 10
They are present and stable:	1 2 3 4 5 6 7 8 9 10
They are concerned about student achievement:	1 2 3 4 5 6 7 8 9 10
They feel a sense of belonging to the school:	1 2 3 4 5 6 7 8 9 10

Total Score for Question 3	

If your score is

- *higher than 80,* the mobilization of your staff is *very good.*
- *between 50 and 79,* the mobilization of your staff is *average.*
- *less than 49,* the mobilization of your staff is *low.*

Based on my results, what actions should I undertake to improve the mobiliza-tion of my staff?

Method

5.2.5 — Objectively Analyze the School's Climate

💬 *What the Supervisors Say*

One supervisor in our study analyzed their school's climate:

- "I love coming to work in my school because the climate is really good. The people who work here are happy too. The level of motivation here is sky high." (Principal, Elementary)

Another supervisor conducted a self-evaluation of their ability to analyze the climate:

- "My ability to analyze helps me to see things rapidly. . . . An ability to analyze, to summarize, so I can quickly identify what the problem is and what the solutions are . . . what measures I need to introduce." (Principal, Adult Education)

To promote and maintain a healthy climate, supervisors proposed several strategies:

- "In my individual interviews, I put the teacher at ease through my demeanor, my gestures. In my group meetings, I often use humor to relax the atmosphere." (Principal, Elementary)

- "When one staff member constantly criticizes me, is always negative or is a rumor-starter, I always intervene and do it immediately. It's not good for the school's climate." (Principal, Elementary)

How far do these testimonials reflect your experiences? (See Table 5.22.)

✔️ **Table 5.22.   Self-Evaluation: Objectively Analyze the School's Climate**

	Yes	Sometimes	No	Does not apply
1. I analyze the type of relationship between each teacher in the group (level, cycle, department, school-team).				
2. I determine the level of motivation of my teachers.				

(Continued)

Table 5.22. *(Continued)*

	Yes	Sometimes	No	Does not apply
3. I can qualify the type of relationship I have with my teachers.				
4. During my individual and group meetings, I collect data on the climate.				
5. I analyze and identify the climate existing among the students, as well as between teachers, students/teachers, and teachers/parents.				
6. I quickly intervene to resolve an interpersonal conflict.				
I believe that most of my teachers . . .				
7. are satisfied with their quality of life in the school.				
8. are proud of their school and have a sense of belonging.				
9. generally trust each other.				
10. experience interdependence in their work.				
11. grow professionally and are successful in the school.				
12. believe that they are effective and so is their school.				
13. are open to talking about anything.				
Others:				

In light of these answers, how would I qualify my school's climate? Very healthy, healthy, or not at all healthy? What actions should I undertake to analyze my school's climate more objectively?

Table 5.23 contains an exercise to evaluate your school's climate.

How do you explain the gap between the real climate and the ideal climate? What actions should you consider undertaking to bridge this gap and improve your school's climate?

Table 5.24 contains an exercise on the dimensions of organizational climate.

Table 5.23. Exercise—Evaluating My School's Climate (adapted from Tardif, 2005)

Teacher Supervision Model and Practices

For each of the 6 elements of school climate, place an *R* under the number corresponding to your evaluation of your school's *real* climate, and an *I* under the number corresponding to your estimation of what would be an *ideal* climate.

1. *Conformity:* the feeling that there are many imposed restrictions (interior and exterior), rules, and procedures to which we must comply (as opposed to the freedom to organize one's own work); a level of formality in the school.

Conformity is not one of my school's characteristics.	1	2	3	4	5	6	7	8	9	10	Conformity is one of my school's characteristics.

2. *Responsibility:* There is a delegation/decentralization of responsibilities within the group. We can make decisions without constantly referring to a superior. I feel self-reliant and I am capable of being accountable.

No delegation of responsibility	1	2	3	4	5	6	7	8	9	10	Strong delegation of responsibility

3. *Standards:* Importance is placed on teacher performance and quality production. Characteristic of school/organization that establishes challenging objectives and communicates them to their members who undertake actions to attain these objectives.

Nonexistent or weak standards.	1	2	3	4	5	6	7	8	9	10	Standards that are sufficiently high to constitute a challenge.

4. *Rewards:* when teachers feel rewarded for their efforts rather than being reprimanded or criticized for their mistakes. Recognition is part of the process.

The teachers' efforts are reprimanded, criticized, or rejected.	1	2	3	4	5	6	7	8	9	10	The teachers' efforts are rewarded, noticed, recognized.

(Continued)

Table 5.23.   *(Continued)*

5. *Clear organization:* the sense that things are well organized, that the objectives, rules, and policies are clearly defined and not vague.

The group is disorganized; there is chaos.	1	2	3	4	5	6	7	8	9	10	The group is very well organized; the goals are well defined.

6. *Human contact and solidarity:* the sense that friendship has value and is experienced in the school; there is a climate of trust and solidarity. The feeling that work relations in the school are good.

No human contact (warmth) or friendly mutual support.	1	2	3	4	5	6	7	8	9	10	Warm, friendly ambiance.

Interpretation of the Results
Add the ratings over the *R* (real climate) and those over the *I* (ideal climate).
R: *I:*   *Gap between R and I:*

Table 5.24.   Exercise—Dimensions of Organizational Climate (adapted from Tardif, 2005)

CIRCLE the word that best qualifies the statement according to your school's characteristics.

1. *Teachers' positive perception of the organizational constraints.*

   None   weak   average   significant   very significant

2. *Teachers' level of involvement and personal commitment.*

   None   weak   average   significant   very significant

3. *It is possible for teachers to have friendly relationships with peers in the school.*

   None   weak   average   significant   very significant

4. *Teachers have autonomy in their in-class activities.*

   None   weak   average   significant   very significant

5. *Teachers' general level of satisfaction.*

   None   weak   average   significant   very significant

6. *Teachers' positive perception of their salary and social benefits.*

   None   weak   average   significant   very significant

7. *Teachers' positive perception of the challenges given by the principal.*

   None   weak   average   significant   very significant

8. *Teachers' level of trust toward their principal.*

   None   weak   average   significant   very significant

9. *Teachers' level of satisfaction regarding their social benefits.*

   None   weak   average   significant   very significant

10. *Team spirit among the teachers.*

    None   weak   average   significant   very significant

11. *Teachers' sense of pride in belonging to this school.*

    None   weak   average   significant   very significant

Interpretation of the Results
Score 4 points for *very significant*; Score 3 points for *significant*; Score 2 points for *average*; Score 1 point for *weak*

If you obtained a score between
- *33 and 44,* your school's climate is *very good.*
- *21 and 32,* your school's climate is *good.*
- *10 and 20,* your school's climate *needs improvement.*
- *1 and 9,* your school's climate *is in dire need of improvement.*

In light of the results, what actions should you consider undertaking to improve your school's climate?

5.2.6 — Develop and Implement a Pluriannual Supervision Plan for My Teachers

What the Supervisors Say

Planning supervision meetings can be a challenge for many supervisors:

- "In any case, what needs to be improved is my planning of the supervision meetings, that's for sure. Perhaps a bit more consistency . . . I want a three-year plan. I think that it's realistic to spread it out that way. I should work on that more." (Principal, Elementary)

- "What I have to work on in our calendars—which are constantly changing—is the planning and consistency of the meetings that we want to do. We have to reserve these moments in our schedule. But there are always unexpected things." (Vice Principal, Secondary)

Other supervisors made supervision duties and deadlines a priority:

- "Because I can't do everything the same year, I spread out my individual teacher supervision over three years. That said, I do annual supervisions with non-tenured teachers because I don't have the choice." (Principal, Elementary)

- "We are going to give us something that is doable over three years." (Vice Principal, Secondary)

Having a well-planned schedule is all well and good, but the work does not stop there. Supervisors must be accountable and stick to their schedule:

- "Things to work on? Maybe more discipline in my meetings. Sometimes, respecting a meeting plan, respecting the application of what I decided, drawing up a plan, it can help. Sometimes I am not disciplined enough in my preparation of some of the meetings. I sometimes think that I should work on this; it's all in our head." (Principal, Elementary)

Putting the plan down on paper is important so as not to lose clarity of thought during hectic daily duties:

- "You have to write it down. Make a small plan. We can have more general meetings, but sometimes we need more specific activity, so we have to take a few minutes to write down a more rigorous plan for the meetings. When preparing the interviews with the teachers . . . and in the PLC, it's important to be prepared, to have a plan. Discipline and structure. With everything that goes on, we can sometimes forget planning." (Principal, Elementary)

How far do these testimonials reflect your experiences? (See Table 5.25.)

Table 5.25.   Self-Evaluation: Develop and Implement a Pluriannual Supervision Plan for My Teachers

	Yes	Sometimes	No	Does not apply
1. I gather information on the professional development my teachers want.				
2. I develop a teacher supervision plan on an annual or pluriannual basis (depending on the number of supervised persons).				
I supervise, in order of priority . . .				
3. nontenured teachers.				
4. teachers experiencing a problem situation.				
5. newly arrived teachers in my school.				
6. tenured faculty.				
7. Each year, if I cannot meet with all of my teachers, I make sure that the tenured faculty receive feedback on their teaching practice (an individual interview).				
Others:				

What actions should I undertake to develop and implement a structured pluriannual supervision plan for my teachers?

Table 5.26 contains an exercise for your pluriannial supervision program.

Table 5.26. Exercise—My Pluriannual Supervision Program

Indicate, year by year, which levels, cycles, or departments will be affected by your individual supervision plan.

Year 1:

Number of nontenured teachers	
Number of teachers in difficulty	
New teachers	
Number of teachers I will meet with during the year	

Year 2:

Number of nontenured teachers	
Number of teachers in difficulty	
New teachers	
Number of teachers I will meet with during the year	

Year 3:

Number of nontenured teachers	
Number of teachers in difficulty	
New teachers	
Number of tenured teachers I will meet with during the year	

5.2.7—Use Data Collection and Analysis Tools

What the Supervisors Say

Every day, supervisors informally collect data here and there in the classrooms:

- "In our school, it's a given. I go into the classrooms. I talk to the students. I'm not there all of the time. It gives me an idea of what they are doing. It's an unofficial supervision. It sends the message that I'm around, that I can come in at any time. I don't ask permission. But I don't spend all of my time in the classroom." (Principal, Elementary)

Group supervision remains an important method to verify and to perform the necessary follow-ups pertaining to the action plan. Effective supervisors focus on the pedagogical aspects:

- "Monitoring the teams . . . that's how I do my pedagogical supervision. When I meet with the teachers on a regular basis, we look at the action plan, we go over it together." (Principal, Elementary)

As for secondary data, this supervisor uses available data from different sources to plan the action plans for each year. These plans are modified during the year or the following year depending on the needs and the results obtained:

- "The results bring us to develop our action plans and these plans clarify the actions of the cycle-team. And we revise it. At the end of each year, we meet and we look at it. What are this year's results? What are our strengths, our weaknesses? From there, what can we improve? So from there, we change next year's action plan depending on what we found when we met in June. We have the school district results, the provincial results. We also have a bunch of data [on student achievement]." (Principal, Elementary)

These data motivate the teachers:

- "I inverted the mobilization strategy. I want my data to serve as mobilizing agents and not demobilizing ones. When there is a problem, I refer to the data." (Principal, Adult Education)

Students' outcomes make it possible to target the basic subjects that raise concerns and to take action regarding the evolution of a particular issue:

- "The results tell us which specific subject is giving us trouble. So what do we do with this? That's how we are going to improve our practices. It's all connected." (Principal, Elementary)

- "One strength is being able to interpret school data, being able to put a finger on what we need to work on more." (Principal, Elementary)

- "Analyzing the students' results using software is a good way to do it. In addition, I have the parents' observations, the students' outcomes." (Principal, Secondary)

How far do these testimonials reflect your experiences? (See Table 5.27.)

Table 5.27.   Self-Evaluation: Use Data Collection and Analysis Tools

	Yes	Sometimes	No	Does not apply
1. I have the necessary data collection tools.				
2. I know how to adapt these tools to the teachers' needs.				
3. I collect data by targeting certain specific areas that we both agreed on.				
4. I take into account the annual action plan when I collect the data.				
5. I have a list of the failing and/or at-risk students in the basic subjects.				
6. I focus my data collection on the students, among others.				
7. I am capable of analyzing the data I have collected.				
8. I am able to make connections between the results of the collected data and the annual action plan.				
Others:				

What actions should I undertake to collect and analyze data more efficiently?

5.2.8 — Agree to the Mutual Expectations During the Individual/Group Supervision Process

What the Supervisors Say

A good supervisor makes sure that all parties agree to their respective expectations or responsibilities during work group/PLC meetings in preparation for the following meeting:

- "In addition, when I finish a PLC or work group meeting, the 'who does what' is always determined for the next meeting. I have great collaboration from my teachers." (Principal, Elementary)

The fact of reflecting together or reviewing objectives may slow the process down somewhat, but the process allows for healthy discussion:

- "Our progression was less than expected because there was a lot of debate over ideas and basics. It slowed down our progress. I had to reorganize a lot. So we changed our objectives along the way and yes, it did slow us down but it made us talk more about teaching practices. We reflected more on how and why we did things. It turned out to be a healthy process." (Vice Principal, Secondary)

Depending on the situation or the teacher's characteristics, the supervisor may adapt a supervision style, which may at times require being more directive:

- "'I'm sorry. I am setting expectations; I am monitoring you, and that's what I want.' You can say that too. The teacher sees that my objective is clear." (Principal, Secondary)

Because the goal is continued improvement, when a group attains the best performance it can, it may be difficult to do more. In this context, a proactive supervisor may propose qualitative improvements:

- "Last June, we had very good results. I obtained a 100% success rate from my students who transitioned from 6th grade to Secondary 1. The teachers told me 'Next year, we can't do any better!' That's a pretty nice problem to have! Instead of saying what we are doing wrong, let's sit down and talk about what we are doing right. Why are these kids, who come from 60 different countries, who do not speak French at home, how come they succeed? We look at it another way. We can also look at it from a qualitative standpoint." (Principal, Elementary)

How far do these testimonials reflect your experiences? (See Table 5.28.)

Table 5.28. Self-Evaluation: Agree to the Mutual Expectations During the Individual/ Group Supervision Process

	Yes	Sometimes	No	Does not apply
In individual supervision . . .				
1. I ask the supervised teacher to show me their professional development plan.				
2. I explain the aspects to work on based on the school's priorities.				
3. I focus my supervision on the teacher's needs.				
4. the teacher and I discuss and decide on which solutions to use to improve their teaching practice.				
5. the teacher and I identify SMART objectives.				
6. I share with the teacher all of my data collection parameters.				

	Yes	Sometimes	No	Does not apply
7. I provide the teacher with the same data collection grids that I use during the observations.				
In group supervision . . .				
8. I express my expectations to the members of the PLC or work committee.				
9. I listen to their expectations regarding the PLC or work committee.				
10. we collaborate to determine the objectives of the PLC or work committee.				
Others:				

What actions should I undertake so that my supervised teachers and I come to an understanding regarding our mutual expectations?

5.2.9—Guide Each Supervised Teacher to Self-Evaluate and Set Professional Growth Objectives

What the Supervisors Say

Supervisors often mention their teachers' reluctance regarding self-evaluation and setting personal development goals:

- "I ask each teacher to establish their own development goals; it's not easy because some of them always have excuses not to do so, but I insist." (Principal, Elementary)

Those who do succeed in motivating their teachers to determine specific objectives for their professional growth will often review their development action plans:

- "Each team developed their professional development action plan. This action plan is reviewed regularly during the year. It does not sit there on a shelf! So it's encouraging." (Principal, Elementary)

- "Experienced teachers have an easier time self-evaluating. We have to guide our supervised teachers toward this process of regular self-evaluation; it's the best thing a supervisor can do for them!" (Principal, Secondary)

How far do these testimonials reflect your experiences? (See Table 5.29.)

Table 5.29.   Self-Evaluation: Guide Each Supervised Teacher to Self-Evaluate and Set Professional Growth Objectives

	Yes	Sometimes	No	Does not apply
During the preparatory meeting prior to the data collection . . .				
1. I review what professional development has been done thus far.				
2. I guide the teacher to self-evaluate their teaching/evaluation practices pertaining to student achievement and identify which ones they will maintain, consolidate, integrate, or abandon.				
3. I help them identify the priorities they will work on during the year.				
4. I share the observation grid with the teacher.				
5. I ask that my teachers have a professional portfolio.				
6. the teachers show me their portfolio.				
Others:				

What actions should I undertake to bring my teachers to self-evaluate and set personal development objectives?

5.2.10—*Provide Constructive Individual/Group Feedback Following Supervision Activities and Follow Up Accordingly*

What the Supervisors Say

The following supervisors evaluated themselves on their ability to provide positive feedback to their supervised teachers. Some of them were able to not only formulate their feedback based on observable elements but also guide their teacher toward possible solutions:

- "For their strengths, formulate feedback based on facts." (Principal, Elementary)

- "I am able to ask the teacher questions to bring them to find solutions by themselves to solve the issues we discuss." (Principal, Secondary)

This supervisor felt they became too invested in trying to find solutions to their teacher's problem:

- "I have to get better at asking the right questions when I meet with the teacher. I enjoy proposing solutions rather than leading them to find them themselves. . . . But you know the saying: Give a man a fish and he will eat one day but show him how to fish and he will eat forever. . . . Well, it's like that. I listen, and I immediately fall into solution mode in my head. Maybe you could try this, this, or that." (Principal, Elementary)

How far do these testimonials reflect your experiences? (See Tables 5.30 and 5.31.)

Table 5.30.   Self-Evaluation: Provide Constructive Individual/Group Feedback Following Supervision Activities and Follow Up Accordingly

	Yes	Sometimes	No	Does not apply
1. After each in-class observation, I give feedback to the teacher.				
2. After each group meeting, whether it's a PLC or a work committee, I make it a point to provide feedback.				
3. After each individual/group meeting, I ensure or see that someone ensures the appropriate follow-up.				
4. Following my feedback, I make sure that the teacher does the appropriate follow-up.				
5. Following my feedback, I make sure that the PLC/work committee members do the appropriate follow-up.				
Others:				

Table 5.31. Self-Evaluation: Provide Constructive Individual/Group Feedback Following Supervision Activities and Follow Up Accordingly (based on Weisinger, 2013)

Giving feedback	Yes	Sometimes	No	Does not apply
1. Before I give the teacher my constructive feedback, I ask them to self-evaluate.				
I use the teacher's self-evaluation and my data to . . .				
2. determine which behavior I should critique.				
3. determine what is an issue. I point out the weaknesses.				
4. evaluate the best way to present my critique.				
In my feedback . . .				
5. I consider the emotional dimension of the teacher.				
6. I describe the facts without judgment.				
7. we work together on a list of changes to be made.				
8. I determine in advance what I want the teacher to correct so I can tell them during our conversation.				
When I give feedback to the teacher . . .				
9. I give detailed examples to illustrate the problem.				
10. I mention the positive elements throughout our conversation.				
11. I recognize the difficulty of the situation.				
12. I understand that the teacher may have problems.				
13. I am attentive to my nonverbal language (facial expression, body language, etc.).				
14. I discuss the possible solutions.				
15. I repeat the possible advantages of making changes.				
16. I end the conversation on a positive note.				
Following my critical feedback . . .				
17. I do a follow-up with the teacher. I ask them how they feel, whether they have any other questions or if there was something they did not understand.				
18. I evaluate whether the changes are effective and if the teacher is doing well.				
19. I make sure that the teacher holds no anger toward me.				
Others:				

What actions should I undertake to provide constructive feedback to my teachers and follow up more effectively?

Cooperation

5.2.11—Consult School District Services for Specific Expertise

What the Supervisors Say

The supervisors in our study expressed their satisfaction with the human resources services provided to help resolve issues:

- "When I have to deal with a problem situation with an employee, I consult my HR services leaders and am always satisfied with the help I receive." (Vice Principal, Secondary)

A good supervisor recognizes the limits of their expertise regarding education programs and is capable of redirecting their teachers toward the appropriate services for their specific needs, such as an issue with the application of a teaching program:

- "I admit it: I am not an expert on what's in every teaching program. When my teachers ask for answers regarding a particular issue encountered in their application of a program, I refer them to the education consultants." (Principal, Elementary)

- "I am a generalist and an educator. I am not an expert in every domain of pedagogical management, so I refer to the district's experts." (Principal, Elementary)

The supervisors emphasize that when consultation takes place, it is important that the role of each actor be clear (principal, teaching and nonteaching staff):

- "Identify the human resources. What belongs to the teachers? What belongs to the principal? What belongs to the non-teaching professionals at the school district?" (Principal, Adult Education)

It is also important to clarify intentions and explain to the teachers the process in which they find themselves, namely, summative evaluation with a course of action or supervision and an objective of professional development:

- "I think you have to inform the persons involved that they are in an evaluation process when we consult with Human Resources services. . . . If we have difficult cases or cases in difficulty, we necessarily collaborate with Human Resources services, and it's more of an evaluation. On the other hand, any other time, it's more professional development, therefore, a process of supervision." (Principal, Elementary)

How far do these testimonials reflect your experiences? (See Table 5.32.)

Table 5.32. Self-Evaluation: Consult School District Services for Specific Expertise

	Yes	Sometimes	No	Does not apply
1. When necessary, I refer the teacher to the school district's experts.				
2. I make sure that the specialized services have addressed the needs of my teacher.				
3. I consult district services for my needs.				
Others:				

In what circumstances would it be relevant to consult district services for specific expertise?

Communication

5.2.12—Communicate Clearly With My Teachers

What the Supervisors Say

When developing their supervision practices, the participants in our study noticed an improvement in their level of communication, which became

- clearer:
  - "The last few years, I have greatly improved my communication skills. I am more clear than I was before. I succeed in being less in my head. I verbalize my intentions better." (Vice Principal, Secondary)
- more articulate:
  - "You have to avoid jumping from one thing to another. . . . The technique where you reformulate what they (have) understood really works." (Principal, Elementary)
- and more focused:
  - "In my communication methods with my staff, I try to be concise, I use clear language and I explain to avoid ambiguity and false interpretations; I get very good results." (Principal, Secondary)

How far do these testimonials reflect your experiences? (See Table 5.33.)

Table 5.33.   Self-Evaluation: Communicate Clearly with My Teachers

	Yes	Sometimes	No	Does not apply
1. I ensure that the members of the school-team fully understand the communication methods in our school.				
2. I check to see how my staff understands the information I share with them (decoding).				
3. I am attentive to the nonverbal language of my supervised teacher.				
4. I actively listen during my supervision interviews.				
5. My messages are clear, articulate, and focused.				
6. I reformulate to make sure that I have fully understood what the teacher has said.				
Others:				

What actions should I undertake to communicate more clearly with my staff?

In the following exercise, in each case, choose the statement that *best describes you in your workplace.* Should you hesitate between several answers, remember that the personal style of communication corresponds to the way *others perceive you* and to the inferences they make regarding your motivations, attitudes, interests, and intentions. *Circle* your chosen answer. Use Table 5.34 to record your answers.

Example

When answering question 1, you may feel that you are persuasive (a), diplomatic (b), focused on results (c), and logical (d), which could probably be right. However, another person who had to choose a group of adjectives to best describe your personality may have no hesitation in saying *a, b, c,* OR *d.*

Table 5.34. Exercise—My Personal Style of Communication in the Workplace
(adapted from Cormier, 1995)

CIRCLE the letter corresponding to your answer for each statement.

	Analytical	Directive	Friendly	Expressive
1	D	C	B	A
2	B	A	C	D
3	A	B	D	C
4	A	C	D	B
5	A	D	B	C
6	A	D	C	B
7	A	C	D	B
8	B	C	A	D
9	C	B	D	A
10	C	B	A	D
11	B	A	D	C
12	D	C	A	B
13	C	D	A	B
14	D	A	C	B
15	C	A	B	D
16	A	C	B	D
17	D	B	C	A
18	C	D	B	A
19	B	D	A	C
20	C	D	A	B
21	B	D	A	C
22	C	B	A	D
23	D	A	B	C
24	C	A	B	D
25	B	D	A	C
Totals				

1. When I am at my best, the person I am talking with might describe me as a person who is . . .
   a. imaginative, stimulating, dynamic, and persuasive.
   b. understanding, encouraging, diplomatic.
   c. practical, centered on results, effective.
   d. logical, rational, systematic, precise.

2. When I must present a project to the school council . . .
   a. I prepare to present my project in a brief and concise manner.
   b. I rigorously prepare, I prepare support documents, I meet with the president, and I try to foresee what objections I may encounter.
   c. I prepare, but I am not worried about the climate within this committee.
   d. I globally prepare because I know I will find the right words to say once I am in the situation.

3. I am the most convincing when . . .
   a. I have enough time to present a solid case.
   b. I have a concrete and realistic objective to propose.
   c. I have an original point of view.
   d. I have the esteem and respect of the persons I am with.

4. When I have to solve a problem, I tend to . . .
   a. obtain sufficient information and consult others to choose the best option.
   b. let the solution emerge from inside me.
   c. rapidly choose the most practical solution.
   d. pick a solution that works for me and one that is acceptable for my staff.

5. When I have to give critical feedback . . .
   a. I document my feedback with precise data and facts.
   b. I formulate my feedback so as not to hurt the other person's feelings.
   c. I find an original way to present my feedback.
   d. I tell it like it is.

6. When I do a presentation . . .
   a. I present all of the important points in a logical order.
   b. I more or less give a show to get their attention.
   c. I focus on the participants' understanding and involvement.
   d. I get right to the point.

7. If I were to have faults, people would probably say that I am . . .
   a. controlling and slow.
   b. undisciplined and excited.
   c. authoritative and impatient.
   d. oversensitive and too worried about others.

8. If I were a painting, people would probably see me as . . .
    a. a picnic in a park.
    b. an impeccable garden of flowers.
    c. a mountain.
    d. an erupting volcano.

9. Answering question 8 felt to me to be . . .
    a. interesting.
    b. a bit ridiculous.
    c. incongruous.
    d. intriguing.

10. In a discussion . . .
    a. I take into account ideas that differ from mine.
    b. I defend my point of view with insistence.
    c. I am relevant in my arguments.
    d. I often present things from a different angle.

11. For me, substantive discussions are . . .
    a. often a waste of time (mind games).
    b. interesting if we address one question at a time.
    c. interesting if people don't take themselves too seriously.
    d. fruitful if people seek to understand each other rather than stick to their positions.

12. In a situation of conflict where I am personally involved . . .
    a. I make compromises.
    b. I cannot predict my reaction.
    c. I find a solution to resolve the conflict.
    d. I wait for the dust to settle.

13. When I witness an altercation between two teachers . . .
    a. I try to bring them to understand each other, to find a solution.
    b. I get personally involved.
    c. I refrain from intervening so as not to worsen the situation.
    d. I try to get them to listen to reason.

14. When I am personally involved in a conflict, the best general reaction mode is to . . .
    a. bring the other person to see the problem for what it is.
    b. analyze the situation with the other person from different angles.
    c. invest a lot of energy toward a viable compromise.
    d. let time do its work.

15. The main interpersonal dimension that I should work on is . . .
    a. active listening.
    b. self-affirmation.
    c. affective expression.
    d. controlling my emotions.

16. When I interact with someone . . .
    a. I make few gestures and I remain calm.
    b. my gestures are mostly harmonious.
    c. my gestures may be awkward.
    d. my gestures are grand and plentiful.

17. When someone shares a personal problem with me . . .
    a. I try to de-dramatize by thinking of another way to view the issue.
    b. I look for a solution.
    c. I listen attentively and reformulate what I have understood.
    d. I ask a lot of questions after getting a full picture of the situation.

18. I am perceived to be someone who . . .
    a. is often unpredictable.
    b. encourages interpersonal relationships.
    c. demands rigorousness and logic.
    d. is very competitive.

19. In my interactions, I often deplore people that . . .
    a. are not conscious enough of their feelings.
    b. speak without thinking first.
    c. lack imagination, creativity.
    d. talk about nothing.

20. When I am stressed, I become . . .
    a. emotional.
    b. impulsive.
    c. much too controlling.
    d. dominating.

21. I defend my ideas . . .
    a. with tact.
    b. with logical arguments.
    c. with enthusiasm.
    d. with emotion.

22. When I have a decision to make . . .
    a. I consider the persons involved.
    b. I opt for the most practical decision.

    c. I consult and try to make the most insightful decision possible.

    d. I trust my intuition regarding school management.

23. When I am listening to someone . . .
    a. I tend to interrupt to give my thoughts.
    b. I try to grasp their point of view and I reformulate.
    c. I listen to them while thinking of something else.
    d. I give them the time to express their thoughts.

24. When I am given critical feedback . . .
    a. I defend myself.
    b. I try to understand.
    c. I ask for proof.
    d. I impulsively react.

25. I have completed the questionnaire . . .
    a. by trying to analyze my behavior as accurately as possible.
    b. by thinking about its scientific value.
    c. in a haphazard way and do not really believe the results.
    d. quickly, without asking myself why.

Interpretation of the Results

If the result in one column is notably higher than those of the other columns, your personal style of communication is pronounced. If, however, your results are almost equal in two columns, certain characteristics of one style are enhanced by the characteristics of another and other characteristics of this style are attenuated by those of the other. Plausible combinations are *analytical/directive*, *friendly/analytical*, *directive/expressive*, and *expressive/friendly*. The combinations of *friendly* and *directive* and of *analytical* and *expressive* are rarer because these two styles contrast each other due to two dimensions (dominance and reactivity).

    Finally, if your results indicate a more or less even distribution between the four styles, you demonstrate a lot of flexibility.

    Because this exercise refers to a personal style of communication, we suggest that you have someone else complete the questionnaire based on their perception of your style.

Short Comparative Summary of the Personal Styles of Communication

- *Analytical:* slow to react, makes great efforts to organize, focused on processes, minimally preoccupied with emotions and personal feelings, uses traditional frames of reference, prudent action, tends to avoid personal involvement, needs truth and relevance.
- *Directive:* quick to react, makes great efforts to control, focused on the task, minimally preoccupied with theoretical analysis and reflection, the frame of reference is the present, direct action, tends to avoid inaction, needs control and results.

- *Friendly:* moderately reactive, makes great efforts to connect with the other, focused on people, minimally preoccupied with formal logic, the frame of reference is the present, supportive action, tends to avoid conflict, needs cooperation and acceptance.
- *Expressive:* highly reactive, makes great efforts to get involved, focused on interaction, minimally preoccupied with routine and conformity, the frame of reference is the future, in the action, tends to avoid isolation, needs stimulation and interaction.

Table 5.35 contains an exercise to evaluate your communication skills.

Table 5.35. Exercise—My Communication Skills (from Cormier, 1995)

The following list presents attitudes and behaviors that favor successful interpersonal communications in the workplace. Proceed with your self-evaluation for each statement by attributing a rating of 1 (very little) to 7 (a lot).

	My evaluation						
	1	*2*	*3*	*4*	*5*	*6*	*7*
1. I am attentive to the nonverbal signs of my staff members.							
2. I seek to understand ideas that differ from mine.							
3. I try to identify the frame of reference of the person I am talking with.							
4. I accurately reformulate what the other person says.							
5. I am comfortable in the world of emotions and feelings.							
6. I enthusiastically accept the suggestions of my vice principals and teachers.							
7. To better understand, I ask for details, for clarification.							
8. I make sure to separate facts from opinions.							
9. If I have trouble understanding, I encourage the other person to explain their thoughts, their point of view.							
10. I provide constructive feedback/criticism when necessary.							
11. I acknowledge the actions associated with behaviors I appreciate and I congratulate.							
12. I am aware of the effects my behavior has on others.							
13. I accept critiquing from others.							

(Continued)

Table 5.35. *(Continued)*

	My evaluation						
	1	*2*	*3*	*4*	*5*	*6*	*7*
14. I openly recognize my mistakes.							
15. I ask the others to be critical and constructive in their feedback.							
16. I adapt well to the persons with whom I interact.							
17. I take the initiative to resolve misunderstandings as soon as they happen.							
18. When I am challenged, I am capable of calmly discussing and getting my point of view across.							
19. I clearly express my disagreement.							
20. I apologize when it's appropriate, without much justification.							

Interpretation of the Results
If your total is

- *between 20 and 50:* It is obvious that you are more comfortable working alone on tasks than having interpersonal contact unless you are being very strict with yourself. There is definite room for improvement.
- *between 51 and 80:* While you have certain communication skills, others are less developed. The fact that you are aware of your limits is an important step to furthering your professional development.
- *between 81 and 100:* You appear to be perfectly comfortable with interpersonal relationships. All that is left is to hone the skills you already have and enrich your repertoire of answers.
- *over 110:* You master all of the communication skills. Bravo!

Self-evaluating our communication skills is not always easy to do, as we have a tendency to overevaluate. Ask a colleague, your vice principal, or a superior to also do your evaluation. The differences between your results and those of the evaluation done by others on your level of communication can subsequently be analyzed. To perform this analysis, it is important the meaning of each statement be clearly explained to the persons involved; however, perceptions depend on the subjectivity of each person.

Ethics

5.2.13—Encourage and Organize Development Activities Based on the School's Needs and Those of the Teachers

What the Supervisors Say

Our participating supervisors were greatly in favor of professional development for their teachers:

- "I use all of the available funds in the PD committee's budget and my teachers agree." (Principal, Elementary)

Furthermore, these school leaders did follow-ups to make sure that each teacher responded to the proposed activities:

- "I meet each teacher who appears to resist the idea of training or who gets very little professional development; I insist that they readjust themselves and I ask that they come to me with a proposal." (Principal, Elementary)

A good supervisor also considers the students' needs as much as those of their teachers and the school when it is a question of professional development:

- "When I give out money for professional development, I take into account the students' needs, the school's priorities, and the teachers' needs." (Principal, Elementary)

How far do these testimonials reflect your experiences? (See Table 5.36.)

Table 5.36. Self-Evaluation: Encourage and Organize Development Activities Based on the School's Needs and Those of the Teachers

	Yes	Sometimes	No	Does not apply
1. I ask each teacher to present their annual professional development plan.				
2. I use all of the available funds in the professional development committee's budget.				
3. I ask the members of my professional development committee to draw up an annual professional development plan based on the school's priorities and the teachers' needs.				
4. I try to establish an agreement with the teachers' professional development committee representatives on each professional development project.				
Others:				

What actions should I undertake to encourage and organize the professional development of my teachers more effectively, based on their needs and those of the school?

5.2.14—Use Differentiated Supervision for Behaviors Related to the Motivation, Commitment, and Professional Competence of the Supervised Teacher

What the Supervisors Say

The supervisors in our study were attentive to how they welcomed teachers to the process before the latter could be influenced by those who were not in favor:

- "The new teachers, you really have to invest a lot with them so as not to let them be swayed by those who are resistant to the project. My priority is the new teachers. It's absolutely necessary." (Principal, Elementary)

For optimal results, effective supervisors apply an approach that fits the teacher's profile. The following supervisors promoted their supervision as professional development to ensure that the teacher entered the process with an open mind:

- "I have to adapt my intervention strategies. I have to say 'Is there something I can do to help you?' I have to adapt my style to their profile. If I say that I am going to collect data to perform teacher supervision, I will be shot down. So I say 'I would like to meet with you to discuss where you are at.'" (Vice Principal, Secondary)

- "Managing personnel, whether they are young, in the middle of their career, or at the end, it's a very interesting challenge for me. I search for complementary competencies." (Principal, Secondary)

How far do these testimonials reflect your experiences? (See Table 5.37.)

Table 5.37. Self-Evaluation: Use Differentiated Supervision for Behaviors Related to the Motivation, Commitment, and Professional Competence of the Supervised Teacher

	Yes	Sometimes	No	Does not apply
I base my supervision on the behaviors related to the motivation and commitment of the supervised teacher. I think about . . .				
1. their willingness to take on responsibilities.				
2. their desire for accomplishment in a specific task.				
3. their willingness to participate in a project (go from inaction to action).				

	Yes	Sometimes	No	Does not apply
4. their tenacity.				
5. their willingness to take the initiative (look for new approaches).				
6. their willingness to make decisions (be self-reliant in their tasks).				
7. their desire to be flexible (adapt to change).				
8. their willingness to become a better teacher.				
Others:				
I base my supervision on behaviors related to the professional skills of the supervised teacher. I think about . . .				
1. their understanding of the job requirements.				
2. their ability to respect deadlines.				
3. their ability to solve problems.				
4. their use of appropriate teaching practices.				
5. their ability to take on responsibilities (establish standards, take risks, consider themselves to be effective, demonstrate self-motivation).				
Others:				

What actions should I undertake to better differentiate my supervision?

5.2.15 — Ensure That the Rules of Confidentiality Are Respected

What the Supervisors Say

Our supervisors evoked the underlying principles of supervision and the necessary relationship of trust and confidentiality, depending on the circumstances.

- "The trust in the supervisor-teacher relationship takes place through discretion." (Principal, Elementary)

- "At the end of a supervision meeting, we both decide what should remain confidential, when it's necessary to do so." (Principal, Elementary)

How far do these testimonials reflect your experiences? (See Table 5.38.)

Table 5.38.   Self-Evaluation: Ensure That the Rules of Confidentiality Are Respected

	Yes	Sometimes	No	Does not apply
1. My supervised teacher and I decide which aspects should remain confidential.				
2. I intervene as soon as the teacher does not comply with the rules of confidentiality.				
3. I am discrete regarding the discussions held during supervision interviews.				
4. I work against every form of gossip/rumor in my school.				
Others:				

What actions should I undertake to ensure that the rules of confidentiality are respected?

5.2.16—*Acknowledge the Personal/Collective Contributions and Successes of My Teachers*

What the Supervisors Say

A successful supervisor is fully aware of the impact they have when acknowledging the positive actions of their teachers:

- "There is no such thing as too little recognition. It doesn't cost anything, so we give it out by the ton where it is deserved." (Principal, Secondary)

- "Acknowledging their progress, it takes energy to do that; they are ready to do that because there is a positive impact, but the little pat on the back, they like that too." (Principal, Elementary)

Some of our participating supervisors admitted that they were spontaneous when recognizing the work of their teachers:

- "I am capable of recognizing people's strengths and tell them." (Principal, Elementary)

- "My strength is acknowledging others. I think it just comes naturally for me." (Vice Principal, Secondary)

Acknowledgment has the advantage of creating discussion and mobilization:

- "It often opens the door to allow us to discuss their practices and acknowledge what has been done." (Vice Principal, Secondary)

- "If teachers are feeling more or less competent, the supervisor's job is to give them confidence. I am a person who can strongly motivate people and mobilize them." (Principal, Elementary)

This appreciation must be expressed on a daily basis without waiting for any extraordinary performance or achievement:

- "It's not spectacular, but it's thanking them on a daily basis. It becomes automatic." (Vice Principal, Secondary)

In some contexts, the recognition may be more formal, such as a ceremony:

- "We had appreciation/recognition activities in our school which were organized by a super committee." (Vice Principal, Secondary)

- "[Teachers] who excel, you know, they're not the ones who need us every day. What they need is to be recognized. A pat on the back, a kind word to tell them they are doing great. So they need my presence because they are happy to show me what they do. . . . Those who do well, I show them my appreciation." (Principal, Secondary)

How far do these testimonials reflect your experiences? (See Table 5.39.)

Table 5.39. Self-Evaluation: Acknowledge the Personal/Collective Contributions and Successes of My Teachers

	Yes	Sometimes	No	Does not apply
1. Every day, I show my appreciation in an informal manner.				
2. I use a variety of ways to communicate my appreciation (handwritten notes; cards; individual or group meetings; informal conversations in the classrooms, corridors, and offices; celebrations; etc.).				
3. I show my appreciation both formally and informally to the members of my PLCs and work committees.				

(Continued)

Table 5.39. *(Continued)*

	Yes	Sometimes	No	Does not apply
4. I organize recognition activities during Teacher Week or at other times.				
5. If there are many teachers in my school, I set up a committee to propose recognition activities for their colleagues.				
6. I tend to recognize the achievements of my supervised teacher rather than to correct their mistakes.				
7. I think that recognition contributes to motivating my teachers.				
Others:				

What actions should I undertake to express greater recognition to my teachers for their personal and collective contributions and successes?

Table 5.40 contains an exercise to evaluate how you express appreciation.

Table 5.40. Exercise—Express My Appreciation (adapted from Savard, 2005)

As you deeply reflect on your behaviors, beliefs, and values, read each of the following statements and place your answer in the appropriate column. When in doubt, choose the answer that appears to be the most representative of your normal behavior.

	Yes	No
1. I have formally identified the strengths and weaknesses of my supervised teachers.		
2. My teachers and I have already directly discussed their main interests outside of work (hobbies, leisure activities, community involvement, etc.).		
3. I know my teachers' work well enough to be able to evaluate their daily successes and mistakes.		
4. I am more inclined to correct my teachers' mistakes than I am to acknowledge their achievements.		
5. I have already officially expressed my appreciation to one of my teachers (e.g., by a phone call, a letter of acknowledgment with a copy in their file, a Happy Birthday card, etc.).		
6. I like to catch people in the act of doing something good.		
7. I treat all of my staff members with fairness.		

8. My teachers, peers, and bosses know me to be someone who easily expresses their emotions and feelings.		
9. I am absolutely convinced that my teachers give me 100%.		
10. I want to hear my teachers' suggested solutions for the issues in our school, and I take these recommendations into account.		
11. I often receive feedback from my teachers regarding the way that I run things.		
12. I believe that personal problems should remain at home.		
13. To be worthy of my recognition, my teachers have to accomplish something truly extraordinary.		
14. Motivation in the workplace comes from within, and therefore, you can't motivate your teachers.		
Add the number of *YES* answers to questions 1, 2, 3, 5, 6, 8, 10, and 11.		
Add the number of *NO* answers to questions 4, 7, 9, 12, 13, and 14.		
Total:		

Interpretation of the Results
- *Less than 5 points:* Recognition is lacking among your management tools. We strongly encourage you to learn more about this positive approach, which will ultimately improve your team's performance.
- *Between 5 and 10 points:* Although it does occur to you to express appreciation toward your teachers, you lack consistency. We strongly suggest that you adopt an approach that will enable you to hone your ability to acknowledge your teachers more often.
- *More than 10 points:* Bravo! You are, without a doubt, a leader who understands the importance of expressing recognition.

5.2.17 — Demonstrate Managerial Courage in Certain Supervision Situations

What the Supervisors Say

The participating school leaders in our study concurred that one of the least-liked tasks was giving negative feedback. However, for the good of their students, it was their duty to proceed:

- "It's the part of my job that I don't like to do, but I have to do it for the students. I would much rather express my appreciation." (Principal, Elementary)

- "When I have to make decisions, it's more difficult emotionally. Being stuck between a rock and hard place . . . making sure people are comfortable and at ease. To have to say 'I made my decision and that's it.' . . . What's also hard is managing conflicts. It takes managerial guts. . . . I am not afraid to tell it like it is . . . but despite that, it is still difficult." (Principal, Vocational Training)

How you "say things" is also important:

- "Don't be afraid to say what needs to be said. Yes, you have to take care *how* you deliver your words, but sometimes you just have to say them and have the courage to say them. Beating around the bush doesn't work. You have to get to the point and say what you have to say." (Principal, Elementary)

How did these supervisors acquire courage over the years? Through experience, of course, but also in their transition over time from complacency to responsibility when they accepted the fact that yes, managerial choices and decisions may translate to not being liked by everyone:

- "Before, I had a hard time being real and saying what had to be said. When you start out you are always worried about not being liked, but I think that ultimately, people appreciate us because they see that we are capable of taking charge, of saying what we need to say. That's what they expect from a good principal." (Principal, Elementary)

- ". . . and courage. I am capable of facing situations and being pro-active. You develop that with experience. Maybe I didn't have the same amount of courage 11 years ago. I am now able to confront, even if the person doesn't want to see my face for a year. . . . You always have to make your decisions based on your students; be just and fair." (Principal, Elementary)

- "When I first began as principal . . . I had more trouble communicating what the problems were. It was something that bothered me, inside, something I mulled over for a long time. Over the years, through my different experiences, I think that you come to see the bigger picture, how relative things are, to look at the changes that have been made. For me, today, you can be straight with me and I will get right on it. That's how I am perceived today, which is good." (Principal, Vocational Training)

This critical view of others obviously requires an ability to question one's own choices and decisions and basically to acknowledge one's own vulnerability:

- "I am, how shall I say . . . humble. I have no trouble admitting when I have made a mistake, nor to recognize when I am the source of the problem. I have no problem proposing improvements for myself. It's not necessarily always the others who are at fault. I take blame when it is due." (Principal, Adult Education)

Negative feedback is sometimes necessary and always important. That said, our participating school leaders emphasized that it is even more important to follow up these negative evaluations so as to *revive* the supervised person:

- "In difficult situations, always make sure you return after a while, maybe the next day, a week later, a month later, make sure to go back and see this person to analyze their attitudes toward you. . . . You can return to see them one week later and tell them 'I passed in front of your class, you're doing ok.' You can 'punish' someone, but the true art is helping them back up. You've just torn down a wall; you have to help them recuperate. People often associate a negative remark with who they are as a person. Knowing *how to be* is not the same as knowing *how to do*." (Principal, Elementary)

- "It's important to intervene, to have managerial courage, because the other teachers see this. If someone goes astray, you have to lead them back. It has a definite impact on the entire group. Also, parents today are not the same as those back in the 1960s. Today, a parent has no trouble telling us that a teacher failed to do one thing or another. Parents rapidly let us know their point of view." (Principal, Secondary)

- "Telling the truth to a teacher isn't everything; you have to explain *why*." (Principal, Secondary)

- "In a supervision interview, when I have to give negative feedback to the teacher, I prepare myself before the meeting, I present them with the facts and I explain my expectations. My experience has shown me that *how* negative comments are presented is crucial. In the end, I make sure that the teacher understands that my comments regard their behavior and not them personally." (Principal, Secondary)

How far do these testimonials reflect your experiences? (See Table 5.41.)

Table 5.41.   Self-Evaluation: Demonstrate Managerial Courage in Certain Supervision Situations

	Yes	Sometimes	No	Does not apply
When giving feedback to the supervised teacher . . .				
1. I determine the aspects requiring improvement as well as my expectations.				
2. I describe the situation without judgment.				
3. I make sure to follow up with a teacher to whom I gave negative feedback.				
4. I am capable of telling it like it is when I feel situations are out of line with school, district, or government policies.				
5. I ask for a second opinion. I get advice before I meet with the teacher.				
6. I clearly express that my negative comments pertain to their behaviors and not to them personally.				
Others:				

What actions should I undertake to demonstrate more managerial courage in certain supervision situations?

5.2.18—Declare My Intentions and Explain My Supervision Actions

What the Supervisors Say

Some of the supervisors in our study declared that clarifying objectives is of paramount importance:

- "From now until June, I explain it and repeat it over and over: My supervision is not an evaluation. I am here to guide you in developing and accomplishing your professional development plan." (Principal, Elementary)

- "I'm going to start talking about my supervision program in August. This year, I intend to launch a teacher supervision and support program so I want to get a head start." (Principal, Elementary)

Others use structured tools shared with the teacher to prepare the supervision interview:

- "I always have a meeting plan divided into 10 sections, with a keyword in each section. It's my notebook, so to speak. I give it to the teacher a week before our meeting. By referring to the keywords, they get an idea of the types of questions I'll be asking. . . . I'll take the time to explain the process." (Principal, Elementary)

When actions are properly explained, it opens the door to effective supervision, as it eliminates ambiguity and helps to gain the other person's trust:

- "Transparency: That opens the door. There is no hidden agenda. This is why I am meeting with you. I am frank in explaining the facts and we begin our discussion, without judgement or interpretation." (Vice Principal, Secondary)

- "Making the other person feel they can trust you, I have that ability. I don't know whether it's my approach or the words I use. . . . When everything goes on with transparency, there are no problems. No one is skeptical." (Vice Principal, Secondary)

Another key component to gaining the teacher's trust in the initial interview is being well prepared:

- "When a teacher comes before me for supervision, what I've always tried to do is get organized as much as possible so that the first meeting goes well, where they understand my expectations, the actions I propose, the number of meetings, whether or not there will be in-class observations, feedback, and all that. My sense of organization and my preparation will help me structure my meetings." (Vice Principal, Secondary)

How far do these testimonials reflect your experiences? (See Table 5.42.)

Table 5.42.   Self-Evaluation: Declare My Intentions and Explain My Supervision Actions

	Yes	Sometimes	No	Does not apply
1. I clarify my supervision objectives with the supervised teacher.				
2. We discuss the measures I plan to use during the supervision.				
3. I share the data collection tools and observation grids with my supervised teacher.				
4. I solicit my staff's collaboration when I develop my supervision program.				
5. I clarify my role in the PLC or work committee meetings.				
6. I explain the feedback I give to the members of a PLC or work committee.				
Others:				

What actions should I undertake to better declare my intentions and explain my supervision actions?

Table 5.43 presents an overview of the main *know how to do* of an effective supervisor. *Can you think of any other pedagogical* know how to do *or* know how to do *in human relations?*

Table 5.43. Synthesis of the Main *Know How to Do* of the Effective Supervisor

	Pedagogical Know How to Do	Know How to Do *in Human Relations*
Leadership	5.1.1 Use pedagogical leadership: Promote my vision of the school system, my educational orientations and values; encourage the professional development of my staff; support pedagogical projects and innovations. 5.1.2 Use situational leadership: Focus on the students' needs and the school's education priorities. 5.1.3 Manage ethnocultural diversity in my school.	5.2.1 Use relational leadership: Encourage communication, consultation, and discussion among the teachers. 5.2.2 Use transformational leadership: Inspire, stimulate, optimize the potential of each teacher, and empower them toward self-reliance. 5.2.3 Delegate support duties and responsibilities to the vice principal and to teachers and closely monitor. 5.2.4 Maintain staff awareness of the main orientations and general objectives regarding student achievement.
Method	5.1.4 Organize my time to make teacher supervision a priority. 5.1.5 Supervise the attainment of the achievement objectives. 5.1.6 Encourage and support the pedagogical projects of my teachers and assist them in their professional development related to the school's priorities and the students' needs. 5.1.7 Supervise the compliance to national/local policies and those of the school in matters of pedagogy. 5.1.8 Financially support my teachers' pedagogical projects and professional development needs. 5.1.9 Structure organization to enable teachers to attend professional development activities. 5.1.10 Perform teacher supervision with no subjectivity.	5.2.5 Objectively analyze the school's climate. 5.2.6 Develop and implement a pluriannual supervision plan for my teachers. 5.2.7 Use data collection and analysis tools. 5.2.8 Agree to the mutual expectations during the individual/group supervision process. 5.2.9 Guide each supervised teacher to self-evaluate and set professional growth objectives. 5.2.10 Provide constructive individual/group feedback following supervision activities and follow up accordingly.

Cooperation	5.1.11 Establish work groups/PLCs in my school and encourage peer collaboration. 5.1.12 Assist my school-team in finding and applying the most effective educational practices for the specific needs of the students.	5.2.11 Consult school district services for specific expertise.
Communication		5.2.12 Communicate clearly with my teachers.
Ethics		5.2.13 Encourage and organize development activities based on the school's needs and those of the teachers. 5.2.14 Use differentiated supervision for behaviors related to the motivation, commitment, and professional competence of the supervised teacher. 5.2.15 Ensure that the rules of confidentiality are respected. 5.2.16 Acknowledge the personal/collective contributions and successes of my teachers. 5.2.17 Demonstrate managerial courage in certain supervision situations. 5.2.18 Declare my intentions and explain my supervision actions.

Chapter Six

The *Know How to Be* Every Supervisor Should Possess

Knowing how to be enables the supervisor to use their personal resources (aptitudes, qualities, emotions, or physiological aspects) in a given situation or context.

6.1—PEDAGOGICAL *KNOW HOW TO BE*

In this section, two *know how to be*s are presented related to ethics:

• Be consistent in my educational values and my professional practice.
• Welcome pedagogical initiatives.

Ethics

6.1.1—Be Consistent in My Educational Values and My Professional Practice

⬜ *What the Supervisors Say*

Effective supervisors act and decide in compliance with their educational values:

• "My decisions and actions must be in line with my educational values; otherwise, it's not long before someone lets me know." (Vice Principal, Elementary)

• "The teachers are always mindful of my expectations. You have to always talk the same talk. When people in the same grade level meet at the end of a term, they know what's coming after the second report card; they know the kind of investigation I'll do regarding the outcomes and the groups. There are less surprises. Things run smoother." (Vice Principal, Secondary)

- "In our network, there is consultation to consolidate our Grade 6 pedagogical practices and assessments with Secondary 1. We also want to ensure continuity, uniformity in our application of prescriptive documents. What are your learning assessment standards and modalities? How many [assessments do we perform] per competency? I have one teacher who has five [evaluations] for one competency while another one has two. Are they equivalent? No. We have results but they're not the same." (Principal, Secondary)

How far do these testimonials reflect your experiences? (See Table 6.1.)

Table 6.1.   Self-Evaluation: Be Consistent in My Educational Values and My Professional Practice

	Yes	Sometimes	No	Does not apply
1. I make sure that all of my decisions are based on the educational values of my school.				
2. I feel comfortable explaining how a decision is in line with my pedagogical beliefs.				
3. I am capable of adjusting myself when someone mentions that I am being inconsistent.				
4. My administrative decisions are based on the values, orientations, and objectives of my school.				
Others:				

What actions should I undertake to show greater consistency between my educational values and my professional practice?

6.1.2 — Welcome Pedagogical Initiatives

What the Supervisors Say

In terms of successful practices, effective supervisors are open to the proposals and initiatives of their teachers:

- "When a teacher comes to me and proposes a pedagogical innovation, I help them to structure, develop, and evaluate it." (Principal, Elementary)

- "I am very open to projects and innovations. They come to me with their proposals. I like it. . . . I wind up supervising in many projects, but I think I'm capable of getting people to believe in themselves and by bringing in the right resources." (Vice Principal, Secondary)

How far do these testimonials reflect your experiences? (See Table 6.2.)

Table 6.2.   Self-Evaluation: Welcome Pedagogical Initiatives

	Yes	Sometimes	No	Does not apply
1. I let my teachers know that I am in favor of pedagogical initiatives.				
2. I always have a small budget set aside to support initiatives that need my help.				
3. I make sure that all of my teachers are aware of their colleagues' initiatives.				
4. I share with my teachers pedagogical initiatives that are going on elsewhere.				
5. I inform my district authorities and the media about the pedagogical initiatives of my staff.				
Others:				

What actions should I undertake to be more open to pedagogical initiatives?

6.2—*KNOW HOW TO BE* IN HUMAN RELATIONS

In this section, nine *know how to be* in cross-curricular competencies are presented pertaining to method (1), cooperation (1), ethics (2), and emotional intelligence (5).

- Be flexible and available.
- Be sociable.
- Be fair.
- Believe in the progress and professional development of each supervised person.
- Possess a strong sense of personal efficacy.
- Manage my stress and emotions.
- Consider the emotional and affective dimension of the supervised person and show empathy.
- Be a good listener.
- Make people comfortable and trusting.

Method

6.2.1 — Be Flexible and Available

What the Supervisors Say

Effective supervisors are flexible and available professionals:

- "I am easy to talk to. . . . I am someone who is very open-minded and always available." (Principal, Secondary)

- "It's easy to come see me; my door is always open. If someone has a question, I will stop what I am doing and listen to what they have to say." (Principal, Elementary)

- "In total, I have almost 800 students. I think that if you want to do this job, supervising, you have to be present. I am there. I have to witness what is going on, to see how it goes. . . . They also need me to be present because they are happy to show me what they are doing." (Principal, Secondary)

How far do these testimonials reflect your experiences? (See Table 6.3.)

Table 6.3.   Self-Evaluation: Be Flexible and Available

	Yes	Sometimes	No	Does not apply
1. I adapt my leadership style depending on what the situation requires.				
2. I feel comfortable changing the way we normally do things.				
3. I often remind my staff of the times I am available to meet with them.				
4. I have an open-door policy with my staff, aside from time used to perform my other duties.				
5. My supervision meetings with my teachers are a priority.				
Others:				

What actions should I undertake to be more flexible and available?

Cooperation

6.2.2 — Be Sociable

What the Supervisors Say   Effective supervisors recognize the importance of being available each day for their teachers:

- "I organize myself to be present with my staff either in the morning before class, during breaks, or at the end of the day after school." (Vice Principal, Elementary)

Successful supervisors tend to be friendly with others, instilling trust and cooperation:

- "I am always in a good mood. I am capable . . . with a teacher who is in a terrible mood, to find the good in this person. I see this as a personal challenge." (Principal, Elementary)

A good supervisor is extraverted, sociable, and confident and can easily connect with others:

- "In human relations, it's easy to connect with people. The way I go about it, my way in is using a lot of humor. It's easy to de-dramatize things and get my message across. It works for me. . . . In my opinion, I'm easily approachable; in my work as principal, I am the boss, that's clear, but when I'm in the staff lounge with people, I will connect with them. If there are people with whom this is difficult, well I give myself the challenge of doing it." (Principal, Elementary)

How far do these testimonials reflect your experiences? (See Table 6.4.)

Table 6.4.   Self-Evaluation: Be Sociable

	Yes	Sometimes	No	Does not apply
1. I am communicative.				
2. I attend the meetings organized by the social committee.				
3. I am confident.				
4. I tend to be friendly with others (smile, use humor).				

(Continued)

Table 6.4.   *(Continued)*

	Yes	Sometimes	No	Does not apply
5. I am easy to be around at work.				
6. I am cooperative.				
7. I am reliable.				
8. I have a sense of responsibility.				
9. I am applied and methodical in my work.				
10. I am capable of maintaining my emotional balance under pressure.				
11. I am emotionally stable.				
12. I am relaxed.				
13. Innovation interests me.				
14. I go to the coffee breaks.				
Others:				

What actions should I undertake to be more sociable?

6.2.3 — Be Fair

Ethics

What the Supervisors Say

Effective supervisors use official documents and data when they are called on to make difficult decisions:

- "I think I am fair. When I feel a bit stuck (it happened with the team this year), I refer to the theory and I find answers in the literature. I know that I am flexible but I also know that the rules are there. For group issues, I try to be fair." (Principal, Elementary)

- "Equity is not the same thing as equality." (Principal, Elementary)

- "Even if I am fair, my expectations in the supervision may vary from one teacher to another because of their training, their experience, and their personality." (Principal, Secondary)

- "Teachers have to accept that our supervision expectations vary from one teacher to another because their needs in terms of professional development and their level of competence are different." (Principal, Elementary)

How far do these testimonials reflect your experiences? (See Table 6.5.)

Table 6.5.   Self-Evaluation: Be Fair

	Yes	Sometimes	No	Does not apply
1. I provide support (material and human resources) based on the individual or collective needs of those I supervise.				
2. My supervision process respects the rights of those I supervise.				
3. I consider myself to be fair in the decisions I make within my supervision.				
4. When making decisions that concern the person I am supervising, I refer to data and to facts.				
5. I know how to differentiate my expectations with regard to supervision by considering the motivation, commitment, and professional competence of each person I supervise.				
Others:				

What actions should I undertake to show greater fairness?

6.2.4—Believe in the Progress and Professional Development of Each Supervised Person

What the Supervisors Say

A good supervisor supports their teachers to the end to encourage their perseverance:

- "When you are in the process, there are times when you tell yourself 'Will they give up?' At the same time, the staff can feel this. You have to support everyone and not surrender. . . . The vast majority of the staff are competent people." (Principal, Elementary)

- "When a teacher shows me that they really do not want to change or improve their teaching, I change my approach, which becomes more directive. Every student has the right to receive quality services." (Principal, Secondary)

How far do these testimonials reflect your experiences? (See Table 6.6.)

Table 6.6. Self-Evaluation: Believe in the Progress and Professional Development of Each Supervised Person

	Yes	Sometimes	No	Does not apply
1. I am convinced that each person can and must progress.				
2. I help teachers who show me that they want to improve.				
3. I give more time to a supervised teacher who has difficulty, but if the situation does not improve, I rapidly intervene.				
4. I use a more directive approach with teachers who do not want to improve.				
Others:				

Under which circumstances do I come to no longer believe in the progress and professional development of certain supervised teachers? What actions should I undertake to avoid this situation?

Emotional Intelligence

6.2.5—Possess a Strong Sense of Personal Efficacy

What the Supervisors Say

"I have a very strong sense of personal efficacy. Challenges do not scare me." (Principal, Adult Education)

Supervised teachers are not the only ones who may feel stressed; supervisors are also susceptible to stress when they begin their duties and when they find themselves in a context that is closed to supervision. Here, assurance comes with experience, and in certain cases, with help from a mentor:

- "The negative leaders in my school took too much room. I needed a few years of experience before feeling confident enough to intervene. The supervision interviews were stressful for me, but over time I managed to overcome this." (Vice Principal, Elementary)

- "Self-esteem is acquired over the years and my mentor helped me a lot in this regard." (Vice Principal, Elementary)

How far do these testimonials reflect your experiences? (See Tables 6.7 and 6.8.)

Table 6.7. Self-Evaluation: Possess a Strong Sense of Personal Efficacy (adapted from Bouchamma, 2006)

	Yes	Sometimes	No	Does not apply
1. The teachers' performance level improves because of the effective techniques I propose.				
2. I know how to convince the teachers to use winning teaching practices.				
3. I have an influence on student achievement.				
4. My teachers obtain a greater level of achievement with their students because of my supervision (which I personally provide or by referring them to the right resources for their needs).				
5. When a teacher does not take my suggestions into account, I know how to approach them to find other ways.				
6. My training and experience give me the capabilities to be an effective supervisor.				
Others:				

Table 6.8.   Self-Evaluation: Possess a Strong Sense of Personal Efficacy

	Yes	Sometimes	No	Does not apply
1. I count on my positive supervision experiences.				
2. I analyze the practices of experienced peers and invest them into my own work.				
3. I create/participate in a community of practice on supervision where the members learn and mutually encourage each other.				
4. I inform my superior of my annual supervision report and explain my successes and the various challenges I faced.				
5. I count on the encouragement of my peers/superiors with regard to my ability to supervise.				
Others:				

Which actions should I undertake to strengthen my sense of efficacy?

6.2.6 — *Manage My Stress and Emotions*

What the Supervisors Say

Effective supervisors are capable of managing their stress by talking about positive things, by taking deep breaths, and by knowing when to take a step back in a given situation:

- "When I feel negative stress, I try and change it into positive stress. For example, if I know that a general meeting will be rough, I tell myself that this will be a positive experience for me that will serve me in the future." (Principal, Secondary)

- "When I feel stressed before an individual supervision interview, I take deep breaths, which calms me down. If, during the meeting, I feel too stressed, I find a pretext to walk out of the room to calm myself down." (Principal, Elementary)

Many supervisors attribute their stress to a lack of time:

- "For me, the lack of time is a huge stress factor because I should deal more with pedagogy. I therefore have to set my priorities." (Principal, Elementary)

How far do these testimonials reflect your experiences? (See Table 6.9.)

Table 6.9.   Self-Evaluation: Manage My Stress and Emotions

	Yes	Sometimes	No	Does not apply
1. I am capable of evaluating my stress level in different situations.				
2. I am capable of analyzing what causes my stress.				
3. I am capable of transforming my negative stress into a positive one.				
4. I am capable of taking measures to lower my stress level.				
5. I am capable of showing my emotions.				
6. I am capable of using relaxation techniques to lower my stress level.				
Others:				

What actions should I undertake to better manage my stress and emotions?

6.2.7—Consider the Emotional and Affective Dimension of the Supervised Person and Show Empathy

What the Supervisors Say

Successful supervisors are caring, responsible supporters who ensure supervision in a climate of respect and integrity.

- "I believe I possess good emotional intelligence. It's there. I am capable, I know that I have it and I am told so. I also have a good sense of humor. Then there's the connection with regard to listening. . . . When you're leading a meeting, things go smoother." (Principal, Secondary)

- "You have to [adapt] what you say, for example, with someone who is highly emotional or has a hard time understanding." (Principal, Elementary)

- "Having self-confidence, being master of the situation doesn't mean taking on the other's problem; otherwise I'd have a ton on my shoulders! I can propose avenues for solutions, put them in contact with resource people to help them solve their problem." (Vice Principal, Elementary)

How far do these testimonials reflect your experiences? (See Table 6.10.)

Table 6.10.   Self-Evaluation: Consider the Emotional and Affective Dimension of the Supervised Person and Show Empathy

	Yes	Sometimes	No	Does not apply
1. I generally show empathy with my staff.				
2. I am attentive to the emotional actions of my staff, and I adjust my actions accordingly.				
3. I apply the principles of emotional intelligence at work (cf. section 4.2.6) that pertain to the situation.				
4. I am capable of managing my staff using either an emotional or rational style of leadership, depending on the situation.				
If my teacher is experiencing difficulties . . .				
5. I place myself in the empathy zone (in neither the sympathy zone nor the retreat zone).				
6. I use the awareness-empowerment approach in addressing the teacher's problem.				
7. I invite the teacher to take the lead; I empower them.				
8. I separate my needs from theirs.				
9. I am capable of confronting them, if need be.				
10. I may use an authoritative role, if need be.				
11. I integrate them into a team.				
To be able to help my teacher in a problem situation . . .				
12. I know my limits and how to respect them.				

(Continued)

Table 6.10. *(Continued)*

13. I respect my zones of vulnerability.				
14. I establish rules of conduct for myself, and I respect them.				
15. I maintain supervision as a necessary tool for discussion and support.				
Others:				

What actions should I undertake to be more attentive to the emotional and affective dimension of my teacher and show empathy?

6.2.8—Be a Good Listener

What the Supervisors Say

Effective supervisors are good listeners capable of understanding those around them by decoding both the verbal and the nonverbal:

- "Listening . . . the ability to really listen to the person sitting across from you. . . . Learn to 'read' the people you work with, to size them up." (Principal, Elementary)

- "I can also read what is nonverbal. You have to listen to what is being said and what you are seeing. It can be developed. Be attentive to the small signs." (Vice Principal, Secondary)

- "My strength is my ability to listen. My ability to receive comments, analyze them, and follow up. It's all connected. . . . When I say 'ability to receive,' I mean that I think that the person feels heard when they say something. . . . I think they come to understand that they are not being judged." (Principal, Secondary)

- "When a teacher talks to me about a problem, I tend to immediately go into solution mode and not just listen to them from start to finish." (Vice Principal, Elementary)

How far do these testimonials reflect your experiences? (See Table 6.11.)

Table 6.11. Self-Evaluation: Be a Good Listener

	Yes	Sometimes	No	Does not apply
1. I rephrase my supervised teacher's point of view into my own words.				
2. When the supervised teacher has finished presenting their point of view, I formulate my opinion of their ideas.				
3. I look at my supervised teacher when they are talking to me.				
4. I encourage my supervised teacher to express themselves either verbally or nonverbally.				
5. I encourage the supervised teacher who hesitates to talk.				
6. I listen to the supervised teacher, even when I anticipate what they are going to say.				
7. I ask questions to clarify ideas/words that I do not understand.				
8. I use short recaps to help my supervised teacher better understand what I am saying.				
9. I forget the distractions around me.				
I am capable of listening to the person talking to me with the same interest, regardless of . . .				
10. how they speak (flow, vocabulary used, etc.).				
11. what I feel for this person.				
12. their context (in difficulty or not, temporary or permanent status, etc.).				
Others:				

What actions should I undertake to development my listening skills?

Complete the active listening exercise in Table 6.12. If you scored less than 70 points, you must seriously improve your listening skills! Here are a few techniques on how to be a better listener (*Mitra Services aux entreprises*):

1. Invest all of your time and be prepared.
2. Make eye contact.

3. Do not talk too much.
4. Put yourself in the shoes of the person talking to you.
5. Ask questions to clarify and recap what you have understood.
6. Do not interrupt and do not anticipate what the other is thinking.
7. Concentrate.
8. Take notes.
9. Listen to the ideas, not just the words.
10. Mention your interest: interject.
11. Put your personal issues aside.
12. React to the ideas, not the person.
13. Refrain from concluding too early.

Table 6.12. Exercise—Active Listening (adapted from MITRA Services aux entreprises)

	Questions	Almost always	Half of the time	Rarely
	Choose the answer that most represents you.			
1.	Do you like listening to other people talk?	5	3	1
2.	Are you motivated to improve your listening skills?	5	3	1
3.	Do you listen regardless of how the person talks or their choice of words?	5	3	1
4.	Do you listen even when you do not like the person talking to you?	5	3	1
5.	Are you capable of listening with the same level of interest regardless of the race, sex, or age of the person talking to you?	5	3	1
6.	Do you listen to your friends with the same level of interest as you do with colleagues or strangers?	5	3	1
7.	Are you capable of forgetting what you were doing?	5	3	1
8.	Do you look at the person talking to you?	5	3	1
9.	Are you capable of zoning out distractions that surround you?	5	3	1
10.	Do you smile or nod your head to encourage the person talking to you?	5	3	1
11.	Do you think about what the person is saying?	5	3	1
12.	Do you try to understand what the person is trying to say?	5	3	1
13.	Do you try to understand why they are saying it?	5	3	1
14.	Do you let them finish what they are saying?	5	3	1

15.	If the person hesitates, do you encourage them to continue?	5	3	1
16.	Do you repeat what they say and ask them if you have understood correctly?	5	3	1
17.	Do you hold on to your opinion of the person's ideas until they have finished talking?	5	3	1
18.	Do you encourage a person who hesitates to talk?	5	3	1
19.	Do you listen even if you anticipate what the person is going to say?	5	3	1
	Questions	Almost always	Half of the time	Rarely
20.	Do you ask the person questions to get them to fully expose their ideas?	5	3	1
21.	Do you ask yourself what the words mean as the person utters them?	5	3	1
22.	Do you make short, silent pauses to help the person better understand what you are saying to them?	5	3	1
23.	Do you feel comfortable when you are listening?	5	3	1

6.2.9—Make People Comfortable and Trusting

What the Supervisors Say

Effective supervisors believe that a relationship of mutual trust is the core of pedagogical supervision:

- "I trust them. The people I work with trust me too. This context is helpful in teacher supervision." (Principal, Adult Education)

In some situations, a climate of trust must first be established before beginning any supervision process:

- "[I had just arrived in my school]. There were other things [priorities] to do in that school before doing anything else. They had to get to know me for trust to begin. . . . The interpersonal relationships were already very difficult. . . . When you have a difficult employee and [you have to fix] the school climate, with a gang of people you do not know, you choose your battles. I was observing; it was not the time to talk about supervision." (Principal, Elementary)

Before supervision can begin, emotions must be taken into consideration:

- "I'm convinced that the first connection you make with someone is through the heart. We get to know each other, we trust each other. After that, we can move forward. . . . If you can't make a connection, it doesn't work. Making that connection with the person is critical." (Principal, Elementary)

Trust is built little by little, over time:

- "This is my second year here. Last year, people were already comfortable coming to talk to me and ask for advice. You feel it when people trust you. It's true. I hadn't thought of that, but they trust me!" (Principal, Secondary)

- "I think that if you want to be able to supervise, you first have to create a climate and a trusting relationship. If you don't want the supervision to be fake, where they only show you the good side, if you want it to be consistent, there is one practice I like to use: I attend the unrelated, nonthreatening activities. You've invited an artist in arts class, I'll go. You're presenting an exhibit, I'll go. I find that people are more receptive. They don't see you anymore as a threat." (Principal, Elementary)

How far do these testimonials reflect your experiences? (See Table 6.13.)

Table 6.13. Self-Evaluation: Make People Comfortable and Trusting

	Yes	Sometimes	No	Does not apply
1. Before a supervision interview, I learn about the teacher's profile.				
2. Before beginning our meeting, I make sure that I adequately welcome the teacher I am to supervise (to relax the atmosphere).				
3. I take time to go over the objectives of the meeting.				
4. During the meeting, if I sense that the teacher is ill at ease or shy, I take the time to clarify the situation.				
5. I use humor to make the teacher feel comfortable.				
Others:				

What actions should I undertake to make people more comfortable and trusting?

Table 6.14 presents an overview of the main *know how to be* of an effective supervisor. *Can you think of any other pedagogical* know how to be *and* know how to be *in human relations?*

Table 6.14.   Synthesis of the Main *Know How to Be* of an Effective Supervisor

	Pedagogical Know How to Be	Know How to Be *in Human Relations*
Method		6.2.1 Be flexible and available.
Cooperation		6.2.2 Be sociable.
Ethics	6.1.1 Be consistent in my educational values and my professional practice.	6.2.3 Be fair.
		6.2.4 Believe in the progress and professional development of each supervised person.
	6.1.2 Welcome pedagogical initiatives.	
Emotional intelligence		6.2.5 Possess a strong sense of personal efficacy.
		6.2.6 Manage my stress and emotions.
		6.2.7 Consider the emotional and affective dimension of the supervised person and show empathy.
		6.2.8 Be a good listener.
		6.2.9 Make people comfortable and trusting.

Chapter Seven

The *Know How to Become* Every Supervisor Should Possess

The supervisor must keep informed regarding reforms and new pedagogical practices, and closely follow how their school navigates through these waters and evolves. Developing their *know how to become* thus represents the first step toward strong pedagogical leadership.

7.1—PEDAGOGICAL *KNOW HOW TO BECOME*

In this section, the following four pedagogical *know how to become*s are examined:

- Self-evaluate and identify my training needs in pedagogy and supervision.
- Learn more about pedagogical innovations and winning trends in this field.
- Develop my professional development program in pedagogy.
- Keep abreast of new theories and practices in teacher supervision.

7.1.1—Self-Evaluate and Identify My Training Needs in Pedagogy and Supervision

💬 *What the Supervisors Say*

The successful school leaders in our study were proud to say that they were up to date on recent advances and training to consolidate their pedagogical role and indicated as an example their participation in this research-action-training project:

- "I am constantly looking for pedagogical training, such as through books, in-class visits, or other ways. It's the same thing with supervision; in fact, it's the reason why I asked to participate in the research-action-training project for school principals in my district." (Principal, Elementary)

One participant explained that by determining their own objectives and professional development needs, they set the example for their teachers:

- "At the end of each year, I decide on what my training needs are for the next year. I must be an example for my teachers." (Principal, Elementary)

How far do these testimonials reflect your experiences? (See Table 7.1.)

Table 7.1.   Self-Evaluation: Self-Evaluate and Identify My Training Needs in Pedagogy and Supervision

	Yes	Sometimes	No	Does not apply
1. I participate in professional development activities to help me in my supervision practice.				
2. I keep informed on innovations in pedagogy and supervision (research literature, discussions with colleagues, etc.).				
3. I establish/participate with colleagues in a PLC or professional practice community on teacher supervision.				
4. I have a professional portfolio.				
5. I am a model for my staff in terms of professional development (I ask of myself what I ask of them).				
Others:				

What actions should I undertake to meet my five training needs in pedagogy and supervision?

See Table 7.2 for an exercise on training needs for group supervision.

Table 7.2. Exercise—My Training Needs for Group Supervision

Determine your training priorities regarding group supervision by identifying FIVE priorities among the following statements.	
Teamwork is an important aspect in a group supervision process. The supervisor must possess certain key skills:	*Order of priority*
1. Learn more on the principles of teamwork: the conditions and requirements; the different forms of collaboration;	
the team's level of maturity;	
the implementation and evolution phases.	
2. Know which resources I can use in a context of teamwork.	
3. Know how the teams of my peers function.	
4. Optimize the work of my different teams.	
5. Get as many teachers as possible to join a work group/team.	
6. Learn more on how to set up a work group/team.	
7. Know what other schools and their districts are doing in terms of pedagogical supervision with groups.	
8. Determine how to improve collaboration among teachers.	
9. Know how my role will change if I choose collective supervision.	
10. Know the benefits of teamwork.	
11. Develop my collaboration with other schools and school districts by participating in work groups/committees.	
12. Know group facilitation techniques.	
Others:	

7.1.2—Learn More About Pedagogical Innovations and Winning Trends in This Field

What the Supervisors Say

The school leaders in our study agreed: To be effective, supervisors must know about innovations and reforms in this field to exercise their pedagogical role:

- "To improve . . . which is pedagogical. Being on top of what's happening—the research, reading—I think it's something I have to work more on." (Vice Principal, Secondary)

While this same vice principal recognized the need to develop professionally and learn more about pedagogy, they admitted their task to be daunting, resulting in a delegation of duties to certain teacher-leaders.

- "I think that for a variety of reasons, that's what we work less on. . . . Of course I would like to be a better pedagogical leader. Be a reference. In a team like [mine], there are leaders. Maybe that's the reason why we delegate a bit." (Vice Principal, Secondary)

Indeed, the supervisors admitted that their pedagogical expertise was limited because they were not specialists in every school subject:

- "Because we are generalists, it's impossible to know everything about every subject in the curriculum. So it's having a general knowledge of learning and evaluation theories . . . on the main aspects of the programs. . . . With the specialists we have in secondary education, it's hard to be a pedagogical leader specializing in only one discipline. Where you become more of a leader is more at the level of their supervision, on the planning, their approach, their practices, and the relationships with their students; you guide them toward self-evaluation. In that sense, the principal is stronger when they introduce approaches and mobilize . . . come to define the contributions." (Principal, Secondary)

Although these supervisors began their career as teachers, their actions in their new duties required adjustments:

- "We were trained in pedagogy to teach; so now, are we still on top of things? Today, with the internet, there are more and more studies." (Principal, Secondary)

- "It really pops! All of this relevant research coming at us from all sides." (Principal, Elementary)

How far do these testimonials reflect your experiences? (See Table 7.3.)

Table 7.3. Self-Evaluation: Learn More About Pedagogical Innovations and Winning Trends in This Field

	Yes	Sometimes	No	Does not apply
1. I am aware of the latest pedagogical trends.				
2. I ask the education consultants at my district's Education Services to keep me informed on the latest pedagogical trends.				
3. I read up on these subjects, and I consult websites.				

	Yes	Sometimes	No	Does not apply
4. I discuss with my teachers who are experimenting with new practices.				
5. I visit the classrooms of teachers who have implemented new practices, and I visit classrooms in other schools.				
6. I participate in conventions and conferences that meet my professional needs.				
7. I ask a teacher who went for training to give me a report.				
8. I ask a teacher who went for training to give a short presentation to their peers on what they learned.				
Others:				

What actions should I undertake to acquire more training on pedagogical innovations and winning trends in this field?

7.1.3—Develop My Professional Development Program in Pedagogy

What the Supervisors Say

A good supervisor recognizes the expertise of their teachers on a daily basis:

- "When parents call me to ask for specific information on learning assessment and evaluation in an education program, I ask the teacher involved to contact them." (Principal, Elementary)

- "We're going to start with the June exam results and we will plan. . . . But I won't plan a supervision calendar but a professional development one. . . . But it goes together. . . . What do you want to change in your class? What is the number 1 factor determining achievement in students who do well? What are your difficulties? Your strengths? As it turns out, Mrs. X said that she also felt that she should work on these aspects." (Principal, Elementary)

How far do these testimonials reflect your experiences? (See Table 7.4.)

Table 7.4. Self-Evaluation: Develop My Professional Development Program in Pedagogy

	Yes	Sometimes	No	Does not apply
1. I created my own professional portfolio.				
2. I use my portfolio to develop and implement my professional development plan.				
3. I recognize the advantages of reflecting on my practice.				
4. I have given myself an annual training plan that meets my pedagogical development needs.				
5. I readjust my annual training plan every year.				
6. I want my teachers to see me as a model for continuing education.				
Others:				

What actions should I undertake to develop my own professional development program in pedagogy?

7.1.4—Keep Abreast of New Theories and Practices in Teacher Supervision

What the Supervisors Say

The principals in our study concurred that professional development in teacher supervision must be encouraged and sustained:

- "After this training I have received on supervision, I will very likely pursue my professional development in this area." (Vice Principal, Elementary)

- "I will continue to read up on supervision and I will be more inclined to discuss my supervision practices with my colleagues." (Principal, Elementary)

How far do these testimonials reflect your experiences? (See Table 7.5.)

Table 7.5.   Self-Evaluation: Keep Abreast of New Theories and Practices in Teacher Supervision

	Yes	*Sometimes*	*No*	*Does not apply*
1. I am interested in this duty as part of the administrative process.				
2. I share my teacher supervision practices with my colleagues, and we discuss new practices.				
3. I read up on teacher supervision.				
4. I consider teacher supervision to be an approach involving discussion and individual/group guidance.				
Others:				

What actions should I undertake to be better informed regarding new theories and practices in teacher supervision?

7.2—*KNOW HOW TO BECOME* IN HUMAN RELATIONS

In this section, a single *know how to become* in human relations is examined: Learn more about human relations approaches.

7.2.1—Learn More About Human Relations Approaches

What the Supervisors Say

Training in teacher supervision must not be limited to the pedagogical aspect but should also include the *human relations* dimension:

- "In teacher supervision, we work a lot in human relations. I want to keep informed on any new approaches on the subject." (Principal, Elementary)

- "I have to be skilled in human relations, because I think that it's the foundation of a collaborative supervision approach between a principal and a teacher or group of teachers." (Principal, Elementary)

- "When I meet with a teacher in the context of individual supervision, my initial concern is to make them comfortable, to establish good human contact: for example, I offer them a coffee and gradually, we get into our conversation." (Principal, Elementary)

How far do these testimonials reflect your experiences? (See Table 7.6.)

Table 7.6.   Self-Evaluation: Learn More About Human Relations Approaches

	Yes	Sometimes	No	Does not apply
1. I am interested in learning new approaches in human resource management.				
2. I consider pedagogical supervision to be a human relations context between the supervisor and the supervised teacher.				
3. My colleagues and I discuss winning human relations approaches regarding teacher supervision.				
4. I ask Human Resources to keep me informed on any new trends on the subject.				
Others:				

What actions should I undertake to learn more about human relations approaches?

Table 7.7 presents an overview of the main *know how to become* of the effective supervisor. *Can you think of any other pedagogical* know how to become *and* know how to become *in human relations?*

Table 7.7.   Synthesis of the Main *Know How to Become* of the Effective Supervisor

Know How to Become Pedagogically	*Know How to Become in* Human Relations
7.1.1 Self-evaluate and identify my training needs in pedagogy and supervision.	7.2.1 Learn more about human relations approaches.
7.1.2 Learn more about pedagogical innovations and winning trends in this field.	
7.1.3 Develop my professional development program in pedagogy.	
7.1.4 Keep abreast of new theories and practices in teacher supervision.	

Chapter Eight

My Professional Development Program in Teacher Supervision Following My Self-Evaluation

Now that you have learned about the skills and practices of an effective pedagogical supervisor and after having conducted your self-evaluation by highlighting your strengths and the areas for improvement, the next important step is to determine *your professional development objectives* to ensure your professional growth as teacher supervisor. The exercise in Table 8.1 is proposed for this purpose.

Table 8.1.   Exercise—My Personal Professional Development Program

My strengths	
Areas for improvement	
My goals	
Actions to reach my goals	

Conclusion

Pedagogical supervision is necessary for any system or professionals who want to improve. Because of the confusion between the concepts of supervision and evaluation, supervision is often rejected or misunderstood, even if this mode of operation ensures the continuous development of teachers. In addition, principals maintain that they lack the time to exercise it.

Based on the results of our research-action-training conducted with practitioners, we believe that pedagogical supervision provides opportunities for innovation and the introduction of new teaching strategies, and generates the most effective teaching practices based on the teachers' needs and those of their school.

Supervision can take different forms. The supervisor is by no means the only expert in the field. The supervisor must indeed manage to share his or her leadership with other teachers and make good use of different modalities of supervision (peer, tutoring, portfolio, etc.).

The supervisor must ensure the professional development of the teaching staff and pursue his or her own professional development (formally or informally and individually or collectively). This statement is in line with recent research on communities of practice as a means of professional development for the supervisor and on PLCs as a means of teacher professional development by peers.

References

Bouchamma, Y. (2005). Evaluating teaching personnel: Which model of supervision do Canadian teachers prefer? *Journal of Personnel Evaluation in Education*, 18(4), 289-308. doi: 10.1007/s11092-007-9025-8

Bouchamma, Y. (2006). School principals' perceptions of personal and professional efficacy with regards to teacher supervision in New Brunswick. *Journal of Educational Administration and Foundations*, 17(2), 9–23.

Bouchamma, Y., Iancu, H-D., & Stanescu, M. (2008). L'évaluation du personnel enseignant au Maroc, en Haïti et en Roumanie: Aimilitudes et différences. *Revue stiinta sportului*, 6(67), 67–92.

Cormier, S. (1995). *La communication et la gestion*. Sainte-Foy, QC: Presses de l'Université du Québec.

Girard, L., McLean, E., & Morissette, D. (1992). *Supervision pédagogique et réussite scolaire*. Boucherville, QC: Gaétan Morin.

Houle, H., & Pratte, M. (2003). Les conseillères et les conseillers pédagogiques. Qui sont-ils? Que font-ils? *Pédagogie collégiale*, 17(2), 20–26.

Tardif, N. (2005). Indicateurs du climat organisationnel dans les établissements d'enseignement. Notes du cours ADS 802 Développement organisationnel, Université de Sherbrooke.

Weisinger, H. (2013). *L'intelligence émotionnelle au travail*. Montréal, QC: Les éditions Transcontinental.

About the Authors

Yamina Bouchamma, PhD, is full professor in the Department of Foundations and Practices in Education at Université Laval. Her academic activities, research interests, and publications notably regard the competencies of school administrators and pedagogical supervision.

Marc Giguère, MEd, is lecturer in the Department of Foundations and Practices in Education at Université Laval. He has extensive experience as principal in both primary and secondary education. His expertise also includes the professional development of school leaders.

Daniel April, PhD, serves as research and communications consultant at the United Nations Educational, Scientific and Cultural Organization (UNESCO) for the Global Education Monitoring Report (GEM). He holds masters and doctorate degrees in educational administration and policy studies from Université Laval as well as a BEd in French second-language education.

www.ingramcontent.com/pod-product-compliance
Lightning Source LLC
Chambersburg PA
CBHW080557220326
41599CB00032B/6514